ITEM 023 260 687

D0495007

Learning Resource Centre

Park Road, Uxbridge Middlesex UB8 1NQ
Renewals: 01895 853326 Enquiries: 01895 853344

Please return this item to the Learning Centre on or before this last date
Stamped below:

9/9/14

338. 479

UXBRIDGE COLLE
EARNING CENT

some liked it hot

The British on Holiday at Home and Abroad

Butlin's FOR YOUR HOLIDAY

some liked it hot

The British on Holiday at Home and Abroad

Miriam Akhtar and Steve Humphries

with Ros Belford

First published in Great Britain in 2000 by
Virgin Publishing Ltd
Thames Wharf Studios
Rainville Road
London
W6 9HA

Copyright © Miriam Akhtar and Steve Humphries 2000

The right of Miriam Akhtar and Steve Humphries to be identified as the Authors
of this Work has been asserted by them in accordance with the Copyright,
Designs and Patents Act, 1988.

This book is sold subject to the condition that it shall not, by way of trade or
otherwise, be lent, resold, hired out or otherwise circulated without the
publisher's prior written consent in any form of binding or cover other than that
in which it is published and without a similar condition including this condition
being imposed on the subsequent purchaser.

A catalogue record for this book is available from the British Library.

ISBN 1 85227 950 8

Printed in Italy

Designed by Design 23

Contents

ACKNOWLEDGEMENTS

We would like to thank all the people who have helped us in writing this book and in making the television series it accompanies, with special thanks to Colette Galza at ITV, Rowan O'Sullivan at LWT, Grant Mansfield, David Liddiment, Director of Programmes, and Dianne Nelmes, Controller of Documentaries and Features at ITV, for commissioning and supporting the project. We would especially like to thank David Prest and Frank Barrett for their expert knowledge and the editorial team of Rod Green and Joanne Brooks at Virgin Publishing.

We are also grateful to the other members of the Testimony Films team, especially editor Daniel de Waal and Nick Maddocks, Gill Hennessey, Katherine Nightingale, Mathilde Damoisel, Wendy Scott, Kate Withers, Jude Wright, Kim Cavanagh, Phil Smith, Caroline LeFevre, Clare Jenkins, Maree Came, Leona Coulter, Mike Humphries, Madge Reed, the cameramen Mike Pharey, Steve Haskett, Dave Blackman and the sound recordist Alexis Cardes.

For their advice and their support we would like to thank Mary Parsons, Keith Betton and the staff of ABTA, Professor John Walton of the University of Central Lancashire, Professor Chris Holloway, John Hassan of Manchester Metropolitan University, Rob Perks of the National Life Stories Collection, Jan Faull and the staff of the National Film and Television Archive, Monique Lentier, Martin Dunford, Alexander Moreton-Shaw, Ann-Marie Evans, Andy Kelly, John Ruthven, the Caravan Club, the Ski Club of Great Britain and Charles Wilson for his history of Benidorm.

Finally and most importantly we wish to thank all the contributors who opened their holiday albums and kindly lent us their memories and mementoes.

INTRODUCTION

THE HOLIDAY REVOLUTION

In the last 50 years there has been a revolution in the holiday habits of the nation. Before the last war, a regular annual week or fortnight's summer holiday was largely the preserve of affluent families. Most people had to make do with short breaks on Bank Holiday weekends, daytrips to the seaside or staying with relatives. It was all change in 1948, however, when the implementation of the Holidays With Pay Act finally brought an annual week's holiday within the grasp of the vast majority of the population. This legislation launched the final heyday of the British seaside holiday with a mass exodus of millions every year who were thrilled to be beside the sea after the agony and deprivation of five years of war.

A second revolution occurred in holidaymaking from the 1950s onwards with the move from holidays at home to holidays abroad. The war had broadened horizons especially for thousands of soldiers who served on the Continent. More importantly the advent of the jet aircraft and cheap package holiday abroad enabled the nation to embark on an annual migration overseas in search of a sunny climate. The sun replaced the sea as the main holiday attraction. A health-giving dip in the cold sea and a walk in the bracing sea air, enjoyed by generations was now relegated to a poor, second best by the new cult of sunbathing. By the 1990s, when four weeks' paid holiday a year was the norm, seven out of ten Britons were enjoying a holiday overseas, many jetting off on package holidays in the sun to destinations like the Spanish coast, Majorca and the Greek Islands. An annual foreign holiday and a summer suntan to match were by then taken for granted as an unexceptional feature of a more affluent, modern life. The simple pleasures of a few days beside the sea in Britain had been replaced by the lure of longer, hotter holidays in more exotic resorts, organised by the ever-expanding international tourist industry; the largest industry in the world.

Another huge change was the move from communal to individual holidays. In the 1950s group holidays, involving extended families, streets, factories or even whole towns were still the norm. During Wakes Weeks in northern industrial towns like Burnley, Blackburn and Bury, there was a mass exodus to the coast as entire communities holidayed together at the same time and at the same resort. Blackpool was by far and away the most popular destination. There was a similar tradition in the East End of London, which emptied every autumn for a raucous, working holiday in the Kentish hopfields. The post-war spirit of community and

Crowds of (heavily clad) sunbathers in Blackpool, summer 1939.

THE HOLIDAY REVOLUTION

camaraderie, and the determination of British holidaymakers to have a good time, was expressed most vividly in the huge popularity of commercial holiday camps. By the end of the 20th century, the trend was for families to holiday by themselves. Many older teenage children and young people were themselves going on independent holidays with their friends rather than their relations. It was all a far cry from the old-style seaside holidays in Britain, first established in Victorian times, where extended families returned year after year to the same boarding house in the same resorts.

In this book, and the television series it accompanies, we draw on a vast range of sources including holiday histories, old travel trade literature and a variety of professional photographs and amateur holiday snaps. Most importantly, we make extensive use of personal testimony to tell the story of the British on holiday at home and abroad, in the words of the holidaymakers themselves. Through our research we have collected stories from almost two thousand people, spanning four generations born between the 1900s and the 1980s, making this the most comprehensive oral history of our national holidays so far attempted. Our main focus is on the 1950s, 60s and 70s, a crucial time in the making of the modern holiday. Most of those we quote initially wrote to us in answer to our call for holiday memories published in the national press and in local newspapers all over Britain. Most of the voices heard are those of around one hundred people we interviewed in depth and filmed for the television programmes. We believe they represent a broad spectrum of the holiday experience of the nation during the post-war years. We hear holiday stories from a variety of period perspectives – from children, teenagers, singles, parents and grandparents.

Each chapter explores a different type of holiday. We hear of the simple bucket-and-spade pleasures, the class snobbery and the sexual excesses of the old seaside holidays in Britain; the fresh air and frolics of the commercial holiday camps; cheap and cheerful holidays in tents and working holidays in the fields;

Beauty and the beasts. Fun at Butlin's Skegness in 1937 with Miss Nottinghamshire (above) and a Tarzan yell competition in 1939.

The new White Star liner, Mauritania II in 1951.

the national love affair with the 'home from home' joys of caravanning; the lure of the Côte d'Azur and the Mediterranean in the early bikini years; the pioneering days of the package holiday; the excitement and glamour of cruising and skiing – holidays once restricted to the aristocracy; and we document the ups and downs of independent youth travel on the hippy trail, hitchhiking, inter-railing, backpacking and partying on the beaches. Our holidaymakers tell of the lure of sun, sand, sex and strange customs.

One theme which emerges in a number of stories is how often innocent adventures and family fun can quickly descend into a holiday from hell. While the appeal of holidays has always been their promise of relaxation, happiness and romance, it is a cruel irony that they have often been extremely stressful and dangerous. This is a consequence perhaps of a growing sense of adventure, going to unfamiliar countries and taking risks, doing things we would never dream of doing the rest of the year, in the pursuit of pleasure. Occasionally the strain of summer holidays – like Christmas – leads to the break up of relationships, which are unable to withstand the pressure of ever increasing holiday expectations and spending more time together as a couple or a family than at any other moment in the year. This is just one aspect of the hidden history of holidays. Through stories like these and many others we try to get behind the popular stereotypes of the Brits on holiday, to unravel the truth about one of our most popular national pastimes.

Official Handbook from Publicity Manager (Dept.S.R.)
Information Bureau. Eastbourne.

FREQUENT ELECTRIC TRAINS · CHEAP FARES

SOUTHERN RAILWAY

BESIDE THE SEASIDE

It was the glorious summer of 1945. World War II, the most destructive war the world had ever known, was over, and it seemed that the whole of Britain was heading for the seaside. For families and loved ones reunited after the war, nothing symbolised the joys of peace, freedom and being British more than the traditional seaside holiday. On the first Saturday of July the trains carried 102,889 people to Blackpool alone, setting an all-time record. For the young, free, single and recently demobbed, a week at the seaside was an irresistible attraction. 'After four years of strict naval discipline, I wanted freedom,' says Ray Rochford from Salford. 'I was in civvy street, I was 21, footloose and fancy free. Meat was rationed, booze was rationed and fags was rationed. The only commodity that wasn't rationed was sex, and I wanted plenty of that. For us young fellas, Blackpool was the Las Vegas of the North. It was Sin City. If you wanted sex with your girlfriend you had to get to Blackpool because there all the shackles and morality dropped off.' For others, the pleasures of the seaside were rather more innocent. 'It was so exciting,' recalls Pat Whittam, a retired teacher from Leeds, 'I hadn't been to Scarborough since before the war, when I was five years old. I lay in bed imagining eating ice cream, looking for crabs in rock pools, building a sandcastle, swimming – just like children did in stories. When we got to Scarborough, Daddy and I built this huge sandcastle, and then we headed for our favourite cafe, but it was boarded up, so we played football there, using the boards as the goal. Lots of the shops along the front were still boarded up but we still managed to find somewhere selling ice creams.'

From the moment in November 1939 when German mines were discovered on the Channel coast, the resorts of the south and east coast had been off-limits. Grand hotels, holiday cottages and boarding houses were converted into billets, barracks, and gun emplacements; barbed wire was stretched along the beaches; mines were buried in the sand and concrete bunkers studded the clifftops. Pillboxes – sometimes disguised as bathing huts or ice cream stalls – were erected on the sand, while deep moats designed to fill with water and trap invading tanks were dug around pleasure beaches. Although the resorts of the northwest were less affected – Blackpool, boosted by a local airbase full of free-spending, high-living, fun-seeking Americans, even experienced a boom – it was only a lucky few who managed to find the time, means or money to get to the seaside during the war.

World War II had interrupted an annual seaside ritual that began back in the 18th century with the new aristocratic fashion for seabathing at 'watering

Opposite: Promenading in Blackpool, 1947.

Below: The only way to eat ice cream.

BESIDE THE SEASIDE

places' on the coast. Hardly anyone could swim in those days and there were no such things as bathing costumes. A new contraption, the bathing machine, was invented in Scarborough to enable the well-to-do to take a therapeutic plunge. For the main attraction of the seaside then was the health-giving powers of sea water and sea air. When the English aristocracy began to visit the seaside they came in winter, believing that submersion in the ice-cold waves, followed by a glass of the seawater mixed with milk or honey, would cure everything from indigestion to nymphomania. When the Prince Regent visited Brighton for the first time in 1783, seeking a sea cure for his goitre, he found himself sharing the beach with pigs rooting for rotting fish heads. He set about transforming the place, commissioning the world's first pier and employing his lover's husband, John Nash, to design elegant terraces, a grand seafront promenade and, most startling of all, the Royal Pavilion, an oriental fantasy straight out of the *Arabian Nights*. In no time at all Brighton was the most fashionable and exclusive town in Britain. Where royalty and the aristocracy went, the nouveau riche followed,

Above: Brighton Pavilion, the fantasy palace designed by John Nash for the Prince Regent as part of the prince's plans to transform the sleepy seaside town.

Left: Victorian holidaymakers enjoy Bournemouth Pier around 1899.

and before long Brighton was overrun, as Queen Victoria put it, with 'flashy vulgarians'. It was a similar story in the other English resorts, and soon the frail, cure-seeking lords and ladies of Margate, Scarborough and Weymouth were in retreat from the pleasure-seeking, husband-hunting, dowry-tracking offspring of merchants, farmers, cloth manufacturers and bankers.

The popular seaside holiday, however, was a Victorian creation, made possible by the railways built to connect urban Britain with the coast. The railway transformed sleepy coastal villages into booming seaside towns and by the 1880s hundreds of miles of sandy-beached coastline had been linked to the industrial towns by rail. Though unquestionably good for the constitution of the Victorian visitors the seaside was no longer primarily seen as a health resort. Now they were chiefly entertainment centres at the end of a railway line with a captive audience who spent all their time and money in one place. The larger resorts rapidly assembled a great array of the latest entertainments – a pier, a promenade and a pleasure beach complete with Punch and Judy, deckchairs and donkey rides – that have now come to epitomise the period charm and bucket-and-spade pleasures of a Victorian family seaside holiday.

To begin with the holidaymakers were mostly middle class. Only they could afford the expensive train fares and seaside accommodation. But by late Victorian times working-class families were also flocking to the coast from the industrial towns and cities. Although there was certainly poverty, there were also many – particularly in the cotton mill towns of Lancashire – who earned a decent, regular wage. With seaside

Below: Bathing machines afforded some privacy for changing and allowed the overdressed Victorian swimmers the dignity of entering the water gracefully without stumbling through breaking waves or shifting shingle. These machines were still in use in 1910.

resorts within a couple of train hours from most big towns, the temptation to escape the slums, the smog, and the slagheap for sand, sea and – if they were lucky – sun, became irresistible. After Blackpool's railway opened in the summer of 1840, connecting it with Preston, Bolton, Manchester and Leeds, the resort received a record number of visitors. Cheap day excursions on summer weekends attracted thousands, who shocked the resort's more sedate visitors with their rowdy behaviour, heavy drinking and habit

TOWN HALL, EASTBOURNE.
Enormous Attraction. For Four Nights and Two Matinees.
Commencing MONDAY, MAY 15th, 1899.
Each Evening at 8, ordinary doors open at 7.30. Grand Illuminated Day Performances on
Tuesday and Thursday, at 3, doors open at 2.30 (equal to night, full performance).
Reserved & Numbered Seats, 2s.; Back Seats, 1s. Children half-price to all parts.
Plan and 3s. and 2s. Unreserved Seats, 3s. (opposite Railway Station), where seats may now
be obtained and reserved.   Early Doors open at 7 o'clock, 6d. extra to all parts; but 3s. and 2s. Tickets
purchased in advance admitted free at the Early Door.

Touring Business Manager ... Mr. WARWICK GRAY. | Advance Agent ... Mr. HARRY RICHARDSON.
Managing Director .... Major BRIAN WILLIAMS

VISIT OF THE WORLD-FAMED
MOORE & BURGESS
MINSTRELS!
DIRECT FROM ST. JAMES'S HALL, LONDON,
In their Unique and Incomparable Entertainments.
Talented 30 Artistes!
Will appear at each performance in a full charming and mirth-provoking Programme of
FUN WITHOUT VULGARITY
During the Visit the Latest London Programmes will be submitted.

Secretary and General Manager...Mr. L. B. BUTLER.
(to whom all communications should be addressed at St. James's Hall, London).

of kicking off their clogs and stripping off their far-from-freshly-laundered clothes for a dip without so much as a nod to modesty. When the middle classes began to boycott the resort's new pier on the days the trippers were there, it was decided to open a second, unashamedly plebeian pier at the cheapest end of town, where admission was half the price, and entertainment was provided by popular dance bands.

Victorian seaside resorts were shaped by social class and their reputation as either upmarket or downmarket became part of the national folklore, continuing into the 20th century and still with some resonance today. While most working-class families enjoyed holidaying among a crowd of other people with lots of modern entertainments, the middle classes generally preferred a more select, quiet, restrained and superior atmosphere away from it all. Some resorts like Southend, Ramsgate and Margate catered for the mass market and the day trippers arriving by coach and train

Above: A quartet of daring Victorian ladies baring their ankles for a paddle at Brighton.

Left: Eastbourne was one of the resorts determined to resist the onslaught of the heavy-drinking, rowdy working classes, even advertising their entertainments as "Fun Without Vulgarity".

Opposite top: Promenading circa 1900 on Eastbourne's Grand Parade with the "bird cage" bandstand and pier in the background.

Opposite bottom: Entertainment on the pier – the Pier Theatre programme from 1929.

from London. Resorts like these laid on music halls, circuses, pierrots, fairgrounds, freak shows and zoos, and provided cheap accommodation to entice people to stay longer.

The pleasures of Margate in 1949 remembered by Josephine Roffey, then nine, were very similar to those enjoyed by children 50 years before. 'In the evenings my mum and dad would want a bit of time for themselves and they'd go out for a drink and give my brother Reggie and me some money to spend on the pier and the amusements to keep us quiet. That was heaven, we'd have great fun, we must have driven the adults mad. I went on the helter skelter but when I climbed to the top I was so terrified I climbed back down again backwards and asked for my money back. The slot machines were lovely, there was What the Butler Saw; my brother wouldn't let me look, he said, "That's not suitable for you", but he had an eyeful, didn't he? But he didn't stop me peeping at all the saucy postcards, I thought they were lovely, what a laugh.'

Many Victorian resorts snobbishly felt that families like Josephine's would lower their social tone and damage their reputation. On the south-east coast, Brighton, Bournemouth and Eastbourne were determined to resist what they

BESIDE THE SEASIDE

regarded as mass invasion by the forces of brash, cheap commercialism. Most resorts made compromises with their social class intake and if they had two or more beaches, part of the resort was allowed to go downmarket while the remainder retained a more refined air. Eastbourne's exclusive status was assured by the Duke of Devonshire who owned and planned much of the resort, refusing any commercial development whatsoever along the seafront. This class consciousness gave almost every resort its own special atmosphere with subtle variations on what has been christened 'snobbery by the sea'. Whilst Margate became cheap and cheerful, its neighbouring suburb, Cliftonville, was more genteel, a cut above. Margate was for generations immensely popular with working-class Londoners, and those wanting to get one up on their neighbours would let it be known that they preferred Cliftonville, actually.

Heather Whittam remembers that this kind of snobbery was still alive and well in Leeds where she grew up in the 1960s. 'As far as my mum was concerned, there was definitely a kind

Above: Donkey rides have long been a part of the traditional British beach scene.

Below: Bathing machines out in force in Scarborough in 1876.

16

Above: Another firm favourite with the kids – Punch and Judy, seen here on Bournemouth's West Beach in 1930.

Right: Unlike today, when almost anything goes, up to the 1950s there was an unwritten dress code for an early evening stroll along the seafront.

Below: World War II defences in place in Bournemouth as seen from Boscombe Pier.

EASTBOURNE, The HEALTH RESORT of the SOUTH COAST.

THE PARADE, EASTBOURNE.- Looking West.

PRINTED FOR THE EASTBOURNE CHAMBER OF COMMERCE.

ATTRACTIVE FEATURES OF EASTBOURNE.
The Empress of Watering Places.

DAILY cricket matches during the season are played at the Saffrons Football and Cricket Ground, adjoining the Town Hall.

First-class coaches and char-a-bancs run daily to Beachy Head, Belle-Tout Lighthouse, Hurstmonceux and Pevensey Castles, Abbott's Wood and Wannock Glen, and to Battle Abbey every Tuesday.

Bands (supplied by the Corporation) play on the sea front, morning, afternoon and evening.

Theatres and other places of amusement.

Beautiful walks and drives. The far-famed Beachy Head (600ft. above the level of the sea) within easy walking distance.

Expansive and velvety Downs.

The facilities for sea-bathing are perfect. The machine accommodation is excellent. Gentlemen are allowed to bathe from the Pier Head from 6.30 a.m. to 9 a.m. There are also large swimming baths for ladies and gentlemen, adjoining Devonshire Park.

Above: Promotional brochure produced for Eastbourne Chamber of Commerce at the turn of the last century.

of pecking order of resorts, and she would use their summer holiday destinations to pigeonhole my school friends. Bridlington was downmarket from Scarborough, Filey downmarket from Brid, and then there were all these little resorts with caravan sites which were basically beyond the pale.'

Where you went and what you did on your seaside holiday was always a potent status symbol and after World War I it became more popular still, boosted by the new health and beauty movement of the inter-war years. Medical examinations of Great War conscripts revealed the perilous state of the nation's health, and doctors began to stress the importance of fresh air, exercise and sunlight. Magnificent Art Deco lidos, some of them modelled on the baths of Ancient Rome, were built, where lithe young athletes encouraged the Brits to get fit with acrobatic diving demonstrations, and restrictions on dressing and undressing on the beach were relaxed to encourage the poor to swim. Only the young were brave enough to don the new, daring unisex swimsuits as they swam, sunbathed and played beach cricket and leapfrog. Most men, like T. S. Eliot's Prufrock, considered rolling up their trousers and perhaps loosening their tie, or exchanging flat cap for knotted handkerchief as they paddled along the shore to be quite daring enough. Fat ladies would tuck their flowery frocks into the elastic of their bloomers and stand ankle deep in the sea to soothe their corns and swollen ankles. Most of the time, however, the Brits on holiday remained fully dressed, sitting, as the poet James Kirkup remembers, on the beach in their Sunday best, picnicking on saveloys, cream cakes and jugs of warm ale.

High on victory, and with a renewed passion for all things English, the seaside holiday boomed in the immediate post-war years as never before. The number of workers with paid holidays had been growing since the late 19th century, but the trend was given new impetus by the Holidays With Pay Act which came into force in 1948. By 1952, two-thirds of manual workers received a fortnight's paid holiday a year. Whereas in the past many working-class families had to be content with day excursions to the seaside, now the majority could afford to stay away for a week or two. Most chose to go to the same resort that they had previously visited on their away days; usually the closest, most easily accessible seaside town to where they lived. One

Opposite top: 'The slot machines were lovely, there was "What The Butler Saw"; my brother wouldn't let me look . . .' – Little Josephine Roffey, on the beach with her family in Margate in the late 1940s.

Opposite bottom: The chicest beach fashions and the new yo-yo craze, 1932.

of the most distinctive features of the classic British seaside holiday of the late 1940s and 50s was the annual pilgrimage to the same coastal area or the same resort year after year. Return visits were especially popular among working class families who had less money and fewer options. The great majority of visitors to the resorts came from a specific catchment area. Blackpool was the Mecca for the textile towns of Lancashire and the North West; much of urban Yorkshire headed for Scarborough and Whitby; the West Midlands favoured the resorts of North Wales like Rhyl and Llandudno, though the more ambitious ventured south to Weston-super-Mare; the East Midlands overwhelmingly chose Skegness and Mablethorpe on the Lincolnshire coast;

Glasgow made for the nearby west coast around Saltcoats; the Welsh valleys headed south for Porthcawl and Barry Island; and Londoners favoured holiday resorts along the southeast coast like Southend, Margate and Brighton.

The most popular resort of all was Blackpool, which, in the 1950s, was visited by seven million holidaymakers each year. In July and August it could accommodate half-a-million visitors overnight. Many came from the industrial towns of Lancashire where wages had been relatively high and where it had long been the norm to close the mills down for a week or two in the summer. Known as Wakes Weeks, these holidays originated in cotton towns of Lancashire way back in the 1890s, and it soon became the tradition for the entire population to head for the sea, leaving their home town utterly deserted. 'Posh' folk went to Southport and Morecambe, the rest to Blackpool. 'Every year in Lancashire there'd be a mass exodus to Blackpool during Wakes Week,' says Ray Rochford. 'All the mill hands and the factory hands had been grafting hard for 50 weeks of the year, so for those two weeks it was heaven for us at Blackpool. We'd be saving up, paying into diddlum clubs and Co-op clubs all year long. It was a great liberation, getting away from Salford and all the smells of the chemical factories, the tyre factories, the glue works, the paint works, the abbatoirs and the breweries.' 'We felt as though we'd been let out of prison,' agrees fellow Lancastrian George Wray. 'We rushed home from work on Friday, had a quick wash, and then headed down to the railway station. When we left, it was like a ghost town; there was barely a shop open.'

The journey by train was, in the era of steam, part of the excitement. To cope with the rush, every summer the oldest, wheeziest passenger trains were brought out of retirement and drafted in to serve the seaside runs. 'Our Wakes Weeks were the last in June,' says Arthur English from Nelson in Lancashire. 'There was a train every 50 minutes, but there were queues all the way down the platform. The crowds were held back until one train had left, and then six or seven hundred more were allowed onto the platform to wait for the next train. They'd be nine deep.'

'Us lads from Salford,' says Ray Rochford, 'would commandeer the last two coaches of the train. We'd pile in there with our girlfriends, lean out of the window and put all our coats and that on the racks, so if anybody came along we'd say, "it's all full up, love," see, we didn't want kids and families in. When we moved off, that was the time for passion, not full sex with intercourse, but heavy petting and kissing. They called it the passion wagon.'

Barbara Holman was another passion wagon regular as a teenager in the 1950s. 'There was a lot of slap and tickle, but that was it. One time I was sitting opposite this boy who looked like Scott Brady, my favourite film star of the time. Gradually I flirted with him, and in the end he asked me if he could see me safely out of the station. That was the man I eventually married.'

Going away to the big resorts like Blackpool was a communal, tribal experience, an annual bonding and celebration for mills, factories, streets and extended working-class families.

Says Arthur English, 'You went to Blackpool to bump into people you knew from back home, so that they could see that you could afford a holiday. You met all the

Above: By the 1950s, Blackpool was visited by seven million holidaymakers each year.

Left: Crowds of holidaymakers soaking up the August sunshine on Blackpool beach in 1936.

BESIDE THE SEASIDE

people you knew from the mills, and large footie teams would form of one mill against the other.

'The beach was so crowded you could hardly see a speck of sand.'

Ray Rochford remembers 'It was the era of big families, eight, nine, ten in one family. Whole streets would go together, Ben Street, Wood Street, they'd stake out their territory on the beach, and they'd all get digs next door to each other. They had this fear of strange places, you see, they lived in such tight communities, and everyone knew each other's business, and everyone felt safe, it was a tribal thing.'

For 50s children the simple joys of a bucket and spade holiday, little changed since Victorian times, were the highlight of the year. 'I looked forward to it from Christmas onwards, counting off the weeks until we'd go down to Dawlish in Devon,' says John Gardner from Bristol. 'I had a red and yellow patterned tin bucket and spade that lasted all my childhood and my favourite thing was building the biggest castle on the beach and watching the tide come in and knocking it down. We'd be in the sea and there would be steam trains going by all the time and everyone seemed to be waving out of the windows and we'd wave back. When it was Friday I was totally miserable and crying when we had to pack up and go home; it seemed such a long time to have to wait until next year's holiday.'

With thousands packed together on the beaches there was a constant danger of

Above: Children were in constant danger of becoming lost on the crowded beaches.

losing young children. This was the greatest concern of parents in the big resorts. Many developed ingenious strategies to avoid such a calamity.

'I was always wandering off as a child so my mother would get this rope and tie me to Cleethorpes pier. I had about 20 feet of slack so I could run around and play. When she'd tied me up she'd go off with Dad and spend a few hours in the pub,' says Gladys Nuttall, 'when I became a parent in the 50s I did the same thing with my daughter, I tied her up to the pier at Cleethorpes so she wouldn't come to any harm.'

More common was the hoisting of flags, usually the Union Jack, to mark out a family encampment. Audrey Witta, a mother on Blackpool beach in the 1950s remembers: 'I'd be there with a great gang of about ten kids, mine, my sisters', my cousins' and a load of village kids as well. So as not to lose them I used to take me Union Jack and stick it on the back of me deckchair so as they could all see it. I took an old school bell as well, one that I'd bought at a jumble sale for two bob, and I'd ring it if the kids weren't coming quickly enough. People'd turn round and give me a look as if to say "what's that barmy woman doing?" but I didn't give a darn, and I never lost one child, not once.'

Bristolian Rose Townsend, visiting Weston-super-Mare with her six children was not so lucky. 'We were making our way across the sands, weaving in and out of the deckchairs, tripping over people's feet, when all of a sudden June said to me "Mum, our John ain't 'ere." I said, "What do you mean, 'our John ain't 'ere'? He was behind you." "He's not 'ere now, mum," she said. I was shaking with fear, and crying me eyes out. I'd never been so worried in all my life.

'This old lady asked me what was the matter, and I told her I'd lost me little boy. "Oh, don't worry," she said. "I expect someone's caught 'old of 'im and took 'im up to the lost children's department." Sure enough, when I arrived at the lost children centre

Above: The simple pleasure of the bucket and spade had barely changed since Victorian times.

BESIDE THE SEASIDE

John poked his head round the door. "Mum, it's me," he said, "I been crying me eyes out for you."'

A much greater danger for the children playing on the beaches was sea pollution. Although resorts continued to sell themselves as healthy escapes from urban grime, the long and little-questioned tradition of disposing of untreated sewage into the sea made some of them a potential health hazard. The problem was greatest in the big resorts like Blackpool where in high season millions of tons of human waste were discharged from pipes close to the beach only to return, barely diluted, at high tide. Even the most appalling pollution was taken for granted by many holidaymakers. Ray Rochford recalls, 'As we was swimming along four or five turds would come floating past, or you might get a mouthful of condoms. We just made a joke of it "Here's another George the Third for you, mate" and just push it aside and carry on. We just thought it was normal.'

Some of the victims of the polio outbreak of the late 40s and 50s, which killed and paralysed thousands of children all over Britain, now believe that they contracted the virus after bathing on polluted beaches. Children who lived near seaside resorts and visited them regularly at weekends were especially vulnerable. Josephine Dingwall

Above: Perhaps as great a childhood danger as becoming lost was the threat from pollution.

24

and her cousin Alex Rowell were among more than sixty polio cases reported in Sunderland in the summer of 1947. They both became ill after swimming on the nearby beaches at Seaburn and Roker. Josephine says. 'When it was good weather our family often used to all go down to Seaburn beach on a Saturday or Sunday. We nearly always went to the same place where there was a big sewage pipe. it stretched from the top of the beach right out into the sea, it was dark green and we used to like playing on it. One day we'd been to the beach and I felt very, very poorly. I couldn't walk and I was creeping up the stairs on all fours. My parents called for the doctor. To begin with they thought it was rheumatism but then it was diagnosed as polio. I was paralysed from the waist down. Basically it's ruined my life. Since then I've been in constant pain. I've always had to walk with sticks or crutches or been stuck in a wheelchair.'

Alex Rowell's experience has chilling parallels. 'We'd always play on the sewage pipes; they were covered in barnacles and we enjoyed balancing on them. walking for hundreds of yards out into the sea and then diving off them into the water. Of course you'd often come up with a mouthful of seawater. It had a nasty taste but you didn't think anything of it. Well. a few days after we'd been to the beach I was struck by a seizure. I began to choke uncontrollably and my face was all contorted. That was the lasting effect it had on me as one side of my face was left paralysed. It killed all the muscles and nerves on the left side of my face. I just feel so angry that this happened to us. All we were doing was what millions of other innocent children were doing at the seaside. And it's blighted our lives.'

Now Alex Rowell and other alleged victims are aiming to sue for compensation from the city of Sunderland.

Ten years later. in 1957. little had improved. Christopher Wakefield remembers swimming with his six-year-old sister Caroline in contaminated water on a beach close to their home near Portsmouth. 'It was revolting. sometimes you could see bits of faeces. toilet paper and condoms floating around in the water. My parents banned us from swimming. but the Chief Medical Officer came out and said there was no danger to health because salt water killed bacteria. So we were allowed to swim again.' In 1957 Caroline contracted polio. 'She had been swimming in the sea and had swallowed a lot of water. She developed a fever and a few months later she died from polio.' Ironically there had been a polio vaccination programme at the time. but because the Wakefields' surname began with W the children hadn't yet had the jab. There was still great reluctance – from government and public alike – to believe that there was anything wrong at all with the good old British sea. Nothing was done. In memory of their daughter. however. the Wakefield family helped to establish The Coastal Pollution League which has played a vital role in raising public awareness of the extent of sea pollution and campaigning for cleaner beaches.

In the 50s. however. such sea pollution did nothing to dent the popularity of particular

Above: Enjoying the sunshine in Southport, 1947 . . .

BESIDE THE SEASIDE

Above: . . . but Eileen Cook's enjoyment didn't always stretch to the boarding house food.

resorts. The habit of returning to the same resort year after year was so deeply ingrained that many would also stay at the same boarding house or hotel. The most popular seaside landladies would proudly boast that most of their clientele had been with them for five, ten or fifteen years. Families looked for a friendly home-from-home atmosphere and avoided risks. 'Every year we stayed for a week in Mr and Mrs Bealey's boarding house in Dawlish' says John Gardner. 'Mr Bealey was a World War I veteran with one leg, he did the cooking and he always seemed to be smiling and laughing. He had a dog that sat under the big table waiting for scraps at mealtimes. Pudding was always prunes and custard and he'd say to me, "Now eat up your black-coated workers and you'll be up in that toilet as regular as clockwork in the morning before you go down to the beach." At the end of the week he'd sometimes let Dad off some of the bill, especially if we'd taken nan and grandpa with us, too. The Bealeys were like one of the family and I remember when he died his wife wrote to us and we were all very upset.'

One powerful incentive to stick with the tried-and-tested was the proliferation in most resorts of overcrowded, sub-standard boarding houses where dragon landladies imposed petty rules and regulations on their guests. In popular mythology the dragon landlady was a red-faced ogre, broad spoken, hair in curlers, feet in carpet slippers and with a husband long cowed into submission. In an era before the development of consumer protection and the grading of holiday accommodation holidaymakers were vulnerable to hostelries that wanted to make easy money during the high season. Bed and breakfast in the back streets of Southend and Blackpool was a cottage industry in which home owners with other jobs packed as many holidaymakers as they could into their spare rooms during high season. The unfortunate families who innocently arrived at such establishments never forgot the experience – and never returned.

'It was 1949, our first ever holiday,' remembers Josephine Roffey from South London. 'My Dad booked us into a boarding house run by a funny old girl called Mrs

Parrott, with a floppy face like a felt hat that I couldn't stop staring at. As soon as we arrived she asked my mum for the ration books, and said to my dad, "If you care to settle up now, I'd be obliged." So, of course, my dad did. Well, when we went upstairs and saw the room, I thought my mum was going to turn round and go home. "I don't know about a boarding house," she said. "it should be boarded up, more like." Us kids, we didn't mind, it was an adventure sleeping in someone else's house but looking at it from my mum's point of view . . . well, one of the beds, the one my brother Reggie and I were sharing, was propped up with a pile of books where the leg had come off. There was a bit of wire hung across one corner of the room to hang your clothes on, the windows wouldn't open, and there was a broken down old fireplace with a jug and basin on it, which my brother had to take down every morning for the old girl to fill with hot water. We all had to wash out of that one jug. My dad had to shave and all, and by the end it was all floating with whiskers. Then there was this beautiful lampshade above our bed. We thought it was lovely, us kids, a beautiful fur lampshade. "Fur lampshade?" my mum said. "Fur? That's thick with bloody dust, that is!"

Mrs Parrott's regime was strict. 'The rules. Oh, the rules! Well, she was very particular about her rules. Had 'em printed out and stuck on the wall, numbers one to ten. Breakfast was at eight sharp and we had to be out of our rooms by nine, no matter what the weather. I don't know why, because she never came into clean. The place hadn't been cleaned for years, and she certainly wasn't about to start now. And we had to be in by ten or the doors would be bolted.' Dinner was at six. 'In the evening she'd bang the gong. This gong was hanging up in the passage and I was dying to have a little bang, you know, because this gong had a lovely sound, but my mum was having none of it. Anyway, we'd go down to dinner, and she'd give us things like bubble and squeak with fishcakes, prunes and custard, tapioca. One night there was suet pudding. Now, when my mum made a suet pudding it was like steak and kidney or bacon and onion. Hers, Mrs Parrott's, had nothing in it at all. It was just plain suet.

Above and below: The British fascination with holidays by the sea has, of course, always extended to boating, too. This is Bridlington in the summer of 1958.

Well, the days went on and it got to Friday night, and we still hadn't had any meat. "I'd like to know what she done with the meat coupons," my brother said. "Bought 'erself a nice joint, I shouldn't wonder," said my dad.'

There were many other landladies like Mrs Parrott whose cooking left much to be desired, as Eileen Cook from Colne in Lancashire remembers, 'We stayed in this awful

XBRIDGE COLLEGE LEARNING CENTRE

BESIDE THE SEASIDE

place in Fleetwood once in the 50s, where we were served tiny portions of corned beef hash with a single slice of carrot. The boiled eggs at breakfast were so small you had to scoop them out of the egg cup in order to eat them. I was so hungry that I ended up spending all the money I'd set aside for entertainment on food.'

Morris Abrahams of Somerset remembers dinner at a Littlehampton boarding house consisting of nothing but bread and marge and a tin of fruit. 'We used to fill up afterwards on fish and chips.'

Ensuite bathrooms, were, of course, unknown. Indeed many boarding houses were blessed only with an outside privy. Josephine Roffey recalls that, 'Mrs Parrott's toilet was outside in the yard and you had to walk through the kitchen to get there, so my mum was always on at us not to make a nuisance of ourselves. There was a pot under the bed to use at night, but that still had to be emptied, which amounted to the same thing. Anyway, my brother would get in at night and say, "Oh, mum, I want to wee," and my mum would clip him round the ear and say, "You've had all day and you wait till now? 'Ave a pear drop to take your mind off it."'

In the 1950s beach etiquette continued in much the same vein as it had before the war, especially among the middle classes. It was only the younger and more liberated generation who wore swimming costumes on the beach. The older generation and the plain old fashioned continued to wear their Sunday best suit, shoes, socks and hat. The taboo on body exposure was still widespread and deeply felt. In the 50s Chris Fawcett was married with two children and worked as a sales representative for a biscuit company in Lancashire. 'At Blackpool I'd always wear my best suit onto the beach. If it was very hot I'd remove my jacket but I'd never take my shirt or tie off or even my hat because it wasn't the done thing. And I'd keep my shoes and socks on all the time even though you really perspired. The more you perspired the better the holiday you thought you were having and I remember people saying, "Oh, I was that hot my shirt was all wet through and I had to wring it out when I got back to the boarding house." Now that was really the mark of having a good time.'

Ray Rochford's next door neighbour was even more restrained. 'Mr Cartwright next door was an overseer at the local mill, and he used to go to Blackpool too. One year we had the hottest summer for 50 years, and there was Mr Cartwright on the beach in his brown suit, brown bowler hat, brown shoes and brown gloves. He wouldn't make no concessions to the weather, you'd never see him with a knotted handerchief on his head or his trousers rolled up, 'cos he didn't want the mill girls to see.'

One of the outstanding memories women have of the 50s British beach is the paranoia about revealing any naked flesh to strangers (or sometimes even to members of the family) as they changed into their swimsuits. 'It was like being a contortionist,' says Odette Lesley. 'I was quite big so I needed a big bath towel draped around me. It was like a tent and somehow you had to take all your clothes and then your bra off, then step into your swimsuit without showing anything. It was very, very difficult; actually it was quite traumatic because if my husband saw anything pop out he'd be very disapproving.'

The taboo was learnt very young as Josephine Roffey remembers. 'People were

so conscious about their bodies in them days, even us kids, you know. We'd be on at mum to hold the towel round us, and not let anyone look. And if the towel slipped, we'd be screaming, "Hold it up, hold it up!" The swimming costumes were really thick scratchy things – I mean, my mum knitted me one once, can you imagine? And they soaked up all the water, so when you came out of the sea they'd be down by your knees, and you'd get all bits caught in the crotch, seaweed and gravel and God knows what else. So it was impossible to stop people seeing your bits wasn't it?'

Most of the exposed bodies were extremely pale and the majority of people had no great aspiration for a tan. 'If you fell asleep on the beach in the hot sun and you'd burnt and gone brown that horrified you,' recalls Brenda Baker from Brighton, reflecting the prevailing attitude of the time. 'You'd think I'm not coloured, I'm British, I shouldn't have this colour, so to be white was still the in thing then.'

Just as the old seaside dress etiquette survived into the second half of the twentieth century, so too did the "kiss-me-quick, knees-up, let-your-hair-down" carnival atmosphere that had been much in evidence in the big resorts since the arrival of the day trippers from the industrial cities in Victorian times. This was a largely working-class tradition and by the post-war years a good holiday meant a week or two of heavy drinking, singing, gambling, fighting – and for the young, romance and a glimpse of sexual freedom.

The seaside had a long association with romance and sex: this was where married couples headed on their honeymoon and where the woman, according to popular myth, was initiated into the joys of sex by her husband – a subject endlessly featured in saucy seaside postcards. On their seaside holidays young people were often in the mood for romance. 'I went to Cleethorpes in 1947 and I met this young donkey man. Buster his name was, on the beach,' remembers Gladys Nuttall. 'I thought he was as smart as a carrot, very handsome, with his red muffler around his neck – he looked a typical gypsy lad with his tan. Well something clicked, we fell in love, and I thought he's the one for me. At the end of the week we arranged to see each other and he came to see me on the train at weekends. Then he said, "It's very expensive, lass, paying out the train fare every week, let's get married." So we did. We'd only known each other three months. But we were so happy. I became the donkey lady working with him and we've done that for more than 50 years. I was Mayor a few years back but I still kept on with the donkeys, and we're still doing it today. We're known as the donkey man and the donkey lady of Cleethorpes. And we still love each other.'

Some resorts had a reputation for sexual excess and by the late 1940s, Blackpool

Opposite top: Chris Fawcett joked that, in the 1950s, a sweat-drenched shirt was the sign of a good day out . . .

Opposite bottom: . . . but by then swimwear was becoming far more prevalent on the beaches.

Above: Gladys Nuttall fell in love with the "donkey man" in Cleethorpes in 1947, married him, and is still there, still in love.

BESIDE THE SEASIDE

The relaxed atmosphere by the seaside led holidaymakers to lose their workaday inhibitions and romance lingered soft and sultry on the sea breeze.

had achieved the status of seaside sex capital. According to Ray Rochford, underneath the North Pier was one of the favourite spots for sex on the beach. 'The girls were just as eager as us, healthy girls, 19, 20, in their prime, and sexually liberated – some of them had been abroad as nurses during the war, so they knew the score. They knew you weren't taking them to Blackpool to buy candy floss. The landladies were dragons, Prussian Guards, so your only alternative was under the pier, where you were protected if it rained. One time there were six of us with our girlfriends – plus about 30 or 40 others – when the beach patrol came along. Two coppers it was, blowing their whistles, and shouting "Come on out of there." And 30 or 40 couples would be there, the guys pulling their trousers up from their ankles, the girls pulling on their French knickers and pulling down their brassieres, all of 'em tripping over as they scarpered, getting a bottomful of sand. We'd wait till the patrol had gone down to the Central Pier, then we'd be at it again, safe until they came back on their rounds an hour later.'

For the next ten years illicit seaside sex reached its zenith in Britain as young people enjoyed higher wages and greater freedom and independence than ever before. The 1950s teenagers in their drainpipe jeans and bumfreezer jackets, twirly skirts and bobby sox, their heads full of rock'n'roll and aspirations fired by American films, wanted more on holiday than a stroll along the pier and a mug of coffee. Many young teenage girls of this generation had sex for the first time on their seaside holiday. 'We'd been courting for two years and we booked two single rooms in a boarding house for a week in Torquay,' says Marjorie Laird from Swindon. 'It all seemed above board, Mum and Dad even came down to see us for the day, I'm sure to check we had separate rooms, but of course we'd planned it otherwise. At midnight when the landlady was asleep Ron would come creep, creep, creeping into my room and we'd spend a lovely night together. You had to make sure nobody knew though or you'd have been in big trouble.'

For many teenage girls, however, it was not a memorable experience. 'I was 15 in 1952 and we'd gone to Brighton for the week,' says Pat Baker from South London. 'Mum and Dad had gone to the pub and left me and my sister by the pier. When they'd gone we secretly put all our make-up on and I got chatting to this well-dressed bloke with a gold medallion, I can't even remember his name. It was getting dark and he invited me off for a walk. We found a quiet spot and did it; it was all over so quickly, and there was no pleasure at all for me, I just thought, "Is that it, is that what I've been looking forward to? Am I really not a virgin any more?" Of course, I didn't tell my mum, I didn't even tell my sister when I got back; they never knew.'

Below: Pat Mancini ran off to Blackpool with her lover and never went back.

Seaside resorts had long provided a safe refuge for married lovers wanting to spend a secret night together far away from the prying eyes of family and neighbours. Usually these clandestine trips to the coast were for one day or one night only, but when Pat Mancini from Manchester went away to Blackpool with her lover in 1967 she never came home. 'I think everyone who's been to Blackpool has done something they should be ashamed of. Well, my marriage had gone wrong, I had two small children

BESIDE THE SEASIDE

and I'd been having a very torrid affair with a musician in a
Manchester nightclub. He said, "Let's go to Blackpool just for
the day," so we went in his car and we were both so madly in
love we didn't want to go back. We just dropped everything and
stayed. It was a shocking thing, the police were looking for us,
but it was so wonderful and exciting being in Blackpool together,
it was like one long holiday. Every day was great, going out on
the sands, going back to this old room we'd booked and making
love. The room was infested with snails and I had snail marks on
my legs but I didn't care. And all we ate was fish and chips.
When our money ran out he got a job on the pier playing the
organ and I was a waitress. And we stayed on in Blackpool. It
had a happy ending, we got married, I sorted out the kids and
we saved up for our own boarding house which I loved running.
And we worked our way up from there.' Nearly 30 years later
Pat and her husband were reputed to be millionaires, running
one of Blackpool's largest seafront hotels.

By the late 1960s however the saucy seaside holiday was
beginning to fall prey to the new, more permissive age. It
appeared rather seedy and old-fashioned. More and more young
people rented flats of their own or lived together openly if they
were so inclined. There was greater acceptance of extra-marital
affairs and divorce as a fact of life. Couples didn't have to scuttle
off to the coast for secret sex as did previous generations. And in
the new era of international air travel and cheap package
holidays, many looked further afield for romance, adventure and
sex – to what has been called the 'Costa del Hanky Panky'. The
sexual legends of Benidorm soon eclipsed those of Blackpool.

The 1960s were in fact a major turning point for the British
seaside holiday. The boom of the preceding decade proved to be not the bright new
dawn that the resorts imagined, but an Indian summer. The cheap, modern package
holiday abroad began to suck the lifeblood from many of the old established resorts.
The new cult of sunbathing and the body beautiful which had begun in the 1930s
really took off in the 60s. The younger generation wanted a guaranteed holiday suntan
to show off back home – which Blackpool and Brighton could simply not guarantee. In
the past the uncertain weather on the English coast had not been too serious a problem
for resorts that traded on their social status, gardens, funfairs and stimulating salt
breezes. There had been a public school stoicism about the British on holiday, which
spurred them on to believe that doggedly overcoming the cold and the rain was in
some way a test of character and positively beneficial to the soul. Nothing would stop
the Brits enjoying their seaside holiday and even trips that turned into disasters could
be recounted amid gales of self-deprecating laughter. The summers of 1954 and 1956
were two of the wettest and windiest on record but the holidaymakers soldiered on
regardless, cheerfully spending more time and money in the amusement parks.

When the established resorts saw the more affluent holidaymakers jetting off in
search of the sun in the 1960s there was no sense of a cataclysm in front of them.

Above: Feeding the gulls, St Ives, Cornwall,
1957.

They simply changed the publicity brochures and began boasting about their sunshine records, practically every one claiming to be the sunniest resort in the land. Eastbourne first made the claim with 1,800 hours of sun each year, then Margate and most other south coast resorts entered the fray. What the brochures claimed was one thing; the actual weather was another. The rain-sodden British holiday became a national joke – but it just wasn't funny any more.

The resorts in the colder, wetter North like Skegness and Cleethorpes were the first to suffer, others like New Brighton on the Mersey went into rapid decline. The beach was washed away, and the main entertainment complex destroyed by fire and never rebuilt. The writing was also on the wall for the Isle of Man, once considered an exotic, glamorous, island destination among northerners. In the 1950s George Wray had saved hard all year so that he could spend his Isle of Man holiday in style. 'Even the voyage there was marvellous. The people so elegant, the captain so dignified and nautical as he walked around, shaking people's hands. I stayed in lovely hotels, and felt like a millionaire. The other guests were so sophisticated and the waitresses wore black skirts and white blouses and served us alcohol at dinner, even though there was still rationing. Everyone used to jazz up their lives – shop assistants pretended to be managers.' By the 1970s the once glamorous hotels in Douglas were beginning to look decidedly down at heel as this island in the Irish Sea lost out to the Mediterranean islands with their guaranteed sun.

In the 1960s and 70s, manufacturing industry in the North was suffering from a sustained recession, the cotton industry was dying and hundreds of mills were closing, all of which knocked the heart out of the ritual Wakes Weeks migration to the coast. One of the major resorts on the north-west coast to suffer the consequences was Morecambe, once a big attraction to many mill towners who preferred it to Blackpool. It was forced to offer cheap deals for pensioners in a bid to fill thousands of unwanted hotel beds – and it was becoming particularly unpopular with teenagers who had no

Above: By the 1960s, young people wanted more than the traditional holiday had to offer – Irene Jackson and friend, June, Isle of Man, 1965.

BESIDE THE SEASIDE

great allegiance to the old Wakes celebrations. 'We were the first children of the post-war generation, and we lived life differently to our parents,' says Irene Jackson of Chorley, Lancashire. 'We had pop music. We had Radio Luxembourg. It was wonderful. What I wanted more than anything was a suntan. There was no way we could afford to go abroad, so I nagged and nagged my parents to let us go to Cornwall. At least there was some chance of sunshine. Did they listen to me? No. And there we were, dragged off to Morecambe yet again, to spend yet another boring holiday in the wind and rain.'

Resorts in the South could reasonably claim around 250 hours of extra sunshine every year compared to their northern rivals. As a result, the one part of Britain which benefited from the new fashion for the sun were the seaside resorts in the warmer southwest. During the 1960s and 70s Devon and especially Cornwall enjoyed an unprecedented boom, with Newquay becoming the centre for the surfing cult, first glamorised on the west coast of the United States. 'If you couldn't go abroad in the 1960s, Cornwall was the next best thing. You just wanted to go to all the beach parties and get off with all those hunky surfers and I certainly did, we had a whale of a time,' says Lynn Hewitt from Taunton.

Old holiday habits were dying fast and the patterns of loyalty which had drawn families to the same resorts year after year were breaking down. From the 1960s onwards there was a new spirit of adventure and many holidaymakers now wanted to

Above: Blackpool has bucked the trend of the decline in British seaside resorts.

experience a different resort each year. Hundreds of thousands of northerners became excited by the idea of a fortnight at Goodrington Sands in Devon or a Cornish holiday at Newquay and St Ives. What made this possible on a mass scale was the rapid spread of car ownership. By 1965 there were nine million car drivers, an increase of six million in ten years. Car ownership would double again by the late 1970s. This gave holidaymakers much more mobility and freedom of choice than ever before. 'We started going down to Devon in the 1960s,' says Barbara Holman from Salford. 'It was so thrilling to do that long journey in our little car, all the way under our own steam. It took all day and we were lucky if we did it in nine or ten hours, but that was all part of the excitement. It was just great to be travelling all together as a family.'

Many chose not to stay at the old boarding houses which once enjoyed a prime position near the seafronts and railway stations. Now families could easily stay further away in the suburbs, in nearby villages or in remote cottages and simply drive to the beach. The old class composition of resorts was diluted even more as working-class families aspired to rub shoulders with their social superiors in formerly exclusive resorts like Torquay. Many also wanted to sample some of the smaller, more remote coastal villages and resorts off the beaten track. Middle-class families who had first colonised the more remote West Country villages before the last war were, by the 1970s, in full retreat, busily discovering new rustic retreats by the sea in Pembrokeshire, Suffolk and Norfolk.

By the late 1960s cars and coaches had surpassed trains as the main form of holiday transport in Britain. But this boom in car ownership brought in its wake traffic congestion and chaos on the roads to the coast and in the resorts themselves. The new motorway network and the M5 link to Cornwall, designed to relieve the congestion only made matters worse in the long run by encouraging a greater volume of traffic. There was growing concern that the car – and the noise, pollution, queues and parking

Above: Blackpool's ever more elaborate illuminations continue to draw the crowds.

35

BESIDE THE SEASIDE

problems it created – was destroying the pretty coastal resorts that the holidaymakers had come to see in the first place. The novelty of long motor car journeys was beginning to wear thin. 'It was 1978 and we were so excited going all the way in the car from Stoke on Trent to St Ives,' says Winifred Gibbons. 'When I was a girl we went to Rhyl every year. This was about 300 miles, but it turned into a nightmare. It took us all day to get there and then we couldn't park anywhere near where we were staying. Every day we were in queues desperately looking for a space to park so we could get out on a beach somewhere, the kids moaning on "are we there yet?" Then it took us a whole day to get back and it seemed we'd spent virtually all the holiday in the bloody car.'

The future pattern of development for British seaside resorts seemed well established by the late 1970s. They were now resigned to being the poor relation of the holiday abroad. More affluent Britons were enjoying four weeks' paid holiday a year and were choosing to spend most of their money on one or two big, expensive holidays abroad. Apart from lack of guaranteed sunshine they were also less inclined to visit the British seaside due to a growing awareness of the health hazards of sea pollution – large stretches of the coastline failed to meet the European safe bathing standards introduced in the last decades of the century. One study in 1995 revealed that every day 300 million gallons of effectively raw sewage was discharged into the seas around Britain and that almost half the coastline was polluted with sewage slicks visible on many beaches.

Nevertheless most middle-class families retained a sentimental attachment to the old seaside resorts. On summer weekends, tens of thousands would spend an awayday at the coast. But they would generally only stay for short breaks of a few days or at most a week. Despite the decline in popularity of the traditional British seaside there were still many families in which at least one parent or grandparent took care to instil a love of its traditional pleasures in the new generation. As Joan Mabey from Leeds put it, 'We have three or four holidays a year, now that we are retired and we go all over the world. But we always have at least a week in Scarborough. We spent our childhood holidays there, and used to take our children there when they were young, and now we take our grandchildren. They love just the same things we and our children did – building sandcastles, exploring rock pools, eating ice creams and fish and chips.'

Working-class families now provided the backbone of the one or two week holiday

Above: Inexpensive foreign holidays offer young families guaranteed sunshine.

trade in many resorts. Yet sadly the very families who dearly wanted to go on a traditional seaside holiday couldn't afford to. The polarisation of poverty and wealth in the second half of the century meant that every year around one in four of all families were too poor go away at all. Having the means to afford an annual holiday became one of the tests of poverty in modern Britain and hundreds of thousands of families consistently found themselves below the poverty line. To add to the problems of the British holiday industry there was also a new trend for booking as late as possible when fine weather was assured and last-minute bargains were on offer. All this seriously dented the economy of many resorts, which, in order to survive were increasingly forced to look to the retired, to elderly out-of-season holidaymakers and to the homeless, dispatched from the cities in search of cheap bed and breakfast accommodation.

Some resorts, however, like Blackpool, have bucked the trend of the late 20th

The beach basks in a foreign sun but the good old British bucket and spade brigade dig on regardless!

century and actually seen their number of visitors grow. For more than a decade Blackpool has marketed itself as a short break destination. With its ever updated attractions, and ever more elaborate illuminations, its appeal has proved to be perennial. Other resorts and stretches of coastline are also enjoying a 21st century renaissance. Cornwall continues to attract huge crowds of young surfers along with its more traditional visitors, the remote coastlines of Suffolk and Pembrokeshire are becoming increasingly fashionable, while renting a beach hut in Whitstable, Kent, has become the latest in chic. These are exceptions to the rule, though, and the resurgence of interest in domestic holidays has a long way to go before it can approach the popularity enjoyed by the British seaside resorts in their heyday.

IT'S THAT MAN AGAIN
AT
Butlin's
LUXURY
HOLIDAY CAMP
FILEY
(Near Scarborough)

Special Visit of
TOMMY HANDLEY &
FULL ITMA COMPANY

In addition to all Butlin's Holiday Attractions

BOOK NOW
FOR
22-29 SEPT.

For booking forms apply:
BUTLINS LTD.
(T.C.O.) 439 OXFORD ST.
LONDON, W.I

OCTOBER HOLIDAY
BARGAIN — FILEY
CAMP REMAINING
OPEN END OF
OCTOBER with all at-
tractions in full swing
Inclusive
Terms £5:0:0 per week

HI-DE-HI

'This is Radio Butlin's calling all campers. Good morning everyone. The time is six o'clock, it's a lovely morning and it's time to get up. We do hope you have a marvellous day in store.'

This chirpy wakey-wakey call started the day for millions of families who chose the holiday camp for their annual break. A cheerful voice would announce that breakfast was ready for the first sitting of campers, whereupon several hundred sleepy campers would make their way from their chalets to the cavernous dining halls to be served a hearty full English breakfast. The campers then embarked on a busy day of communal hijinks. The holiday camp recipe was a huge hit with the British in the decades following World War II. Their golden age was between the late 1940s and the early 60s – in one year, 1948, some 200,000 hopeful holidaymakers tried and failed to make a booking at Butlin's. By the early 1980s it was estimated that one in four of the population had holidayed at Butlin's. And there were very few Britons who had not visited one of the many rival holiday camps which had sprouted up all over the coastline.

Although the holiday camp is fixed in the popular imagination as a post-war phenomenon, immortalised in the hugely popular BBC comedy series *Hi-de-Hi* with its fictionalised 1950s' Maplin's, in fact it has a long history reaching back many decades. Butlin's, Pontin's and Warner's – the most well known names of the commercial holiday camp – first came onto the scene in the 1930s. But well before this there was a tradition of small pioneer camps that appealed to the British desire for fresh air, wholesome food and good, clean fun at affordable prices. These non-commercial ventures knew that camping was a means of getting away on a budget without the expense of hotels or boarding houses and they brought the seaside and the countryside within the reach of the average wallet. The first holiday camp in Britain was the Cunningham Young Men's Holiday Camp on the Isle of Man, which was started in 1894 by a Presbyterian teetotaller from the Working Lads' Institute in Liverpool. Robust boys from all over Merseyside came to join in the team games and organised amusements and to use the heated swimming pool, barber's shop and vast dining and concert halls. They slept in row upon row of

Opposite top: The communal dining halls provided wholesome meals and a shared experience

Above: Regular announcements and the famous wake-up calls came courtesy of Radio Butlin's.

Butlin's
where you make
new friends!

FREE BROCHURE
SEE OVERLEAF

WHATEVER THE WEATHER, IT'S FINE AT Butlin's

candle-lit tents. The format succeeded despite the all-male, non-swearing, non-drinking, non-gambling rules and the fines for breaking the nightly curfew. Mixed and family camps emerged some ten years later. The first one to cater for families along modern lines was the Dodd's Socialist Holiday Camp in Caister which opened in 1906. Camps for workers were pioneered by the labour and co-operative movements offering low cost accommodation, shared facilities and green spaces. The idea was to enhance the quality of life for working people and encourage communal activity in a spirit of camaraderie.

The biggest name in commercial holiday camps, Billy Butlin, built his first camp in

Top left: Cunningham's Young Men's Holiday Camp at Douglas on the Isle of Man.

Above: Many holiday camps, such as Clacton, were temporarily transformed into military bases during World War II.

Skegness in 1936 along the coast from one of his string of amusement parks. This was the showman who brought the dodgem car to Britain from America in 1928. The inspiration for the camps came from a bad experience he had staying in a seaside boarding house on Barry Island in the early 1920s. 'I was astounded by how the guests were treated. We had to leave the premises after breakfast and were not encouraged to return until lunch-time. After lunch we were again made not welcome until dinner in the evening. When it rained life became a misery. I felt sorry for myself but even sorrier for the families with young children as they trudged around wet and bedraggled, or forlornly filled in time in amusement arcades until they could return to their boarding houses.' He resolved to open camps that would look after the 'mass of middle-income families for whom no one seemed to be catering' in a way the seaside landlady had neglected, and to provide all-weather amusements so that rain wouldn't stop play. Skegness was soon overwhelmed with bookings and Butlin opened new camps at Clacton and Filey.

The war brought a temporary halt to the expansion of holiday camps. Many of the camps were requisitioned for military use. 'Enemy Aliens' were rounded up and housed at Butlin's at Clacton before being sent to the Isle of Man or abroad. According to Butlin, 'At first it was intended to be a camp for prisoners of war, and barbed wire had been put up around the perimeter. A row of floodlights were erected and these were kept on all night – beacons in an otherwise blacked-out countryside.' Could this be the origin of all those prison camp jokes? Skegness became a naval training establishment, *HMS Arthur* and Butlin managed to strike a deal with the War Ministry whereby he handed over the camps he was constructing on the understanding that he'd get them back at a bargain price after the war. Pwlheli became *HMS Glendower* and Filey became an RAF camp but not before Butlin had made plans to transform the huge sunken parade ground into a boating lake once the hostilities were over.

After the war the British were in the mood for fun and millions of war-weary Britons were desperate for their first holiday since 1939. Butlin's slogan 'a week's holiday for a week's wage' proved irresistible. There was an air of optimism after the

Above: Refurbished chalets with delightful gardens represented a new start after the war.

war, even though it was still a time of austerity. Brenda Bullock was seven years old when she first went to Butlin's at Skegness in 1946. 'The meals were frugal because rationing was still in force and we ate all the meals off long trestle tables in a large hut that did duty as the dining hall. But we were determined to enjoy ourselves. I loved the chalets with the bunk beds and you reached the top bunk by an exciting ladder. Being able to have our own keys to the chalet was marvellous. The rooms were newly painted in cheerful colours. Little gardens had been planted between the chalets with trellises up which struggled climbing roses. We thought it was all wonderful after the war. Every morning we dodged between the chalets over several neat gardens to our grandparents' chalet to fetch them for breakfast.'

By 1948 one in twenty holidaymakers went to Butlin's alone. The holiday camp's gain was at the expense of the seaside boarding house. People had grown weary of the old-fashioned rules, the lumpy mattresses, queues for the bathroom, 'lights-out-at-eleven' and the grumpy landladies. The holiday camp seemed a much freer way of enjoying the seaside. Roger and Mabel Finnigan stayed at Butlin's in Filey in 1947. 'In a boarding house you had your meals and you went out. You weren't encouraged to stay in, you were more or less pushed out. So all you did was eat and sleep there because there were no facilities, no lounges and a lot of them didn't have their own washing facilities, but in Butlin's we had our own room with our own washbasin, and once the chaletmaid had cleaned it, we could spend all day there if we wished.'

The promise of fun for all of the family, from grandparents to toddlers, was one of the most attractive features of the holiday camp and it was not unusual for three generations of the same family to stay there together. The war had brought about a baby boom and many parents were conscious that their sons and daughters had never seen the sea or experienced a holiday. They wanted to guarantee a good time for their children but also be able

Below: South Sea Islands fancy dress seems to be the order of the day in this picture taken at Potter's Camp, Hopton-on-Sea, 1949

to enjoy themselves secure in the knowledge that their children were safe and being supervised. One of the pioneering and very popular services provided by Butlin's was child listening by the 'night owl' chalet patrols monitored by Radio Butlin's with its regular and good humoured tannoy announcements. *'Hello Campers. This is a very special announcement. Will Mrs Roberts please go to Chalet 16, South Camp, where her baby is crying and the tears are coming out from under the door.'*

Margaret Maudsley from Bradford was a single parent when she took her four children and her mother to Butlin's in the 60s. 'Of course you knew your children were being looked after and compared to seaside boarding houses, where they were always considered a nuisance, this was the first really child-friendly holiday we'd had. The little ones were in bed by seven and the older ones, well, they went out to enjoy everything that was going on; they'd stay up late and watch the shows and go dancing with their grandma and me. It was so big, so free, so lovely and the Redcoats were so kind to them, they just couldn't do enough for you and of course my boys loved it. There were no problems in just letting your children wander off, you knew they'd be fine. My mother used to sit happily knitting and I'd just sit and wait for them, it was absolutely lovely.'

Above: Regular chalet patrols, like this one at Bognor Regis, helped parents to enjoy a worry-free holiday.

At Butlin's children could join the junior Beaver club and many campers fondly remember roller-skating before breakfast, staging shows and making new friends. Every Warner's camp had its own 'Uncle Arthur' whose daunting task it was to entertain the children from dawn 'til dusk. Early each morning he went around all the chalets playing a recorder. Like the Pied Piper he drew the children away from their beds so that they would go off to play and allow their parents a lie-in. Marjorie Chalker from Herts, a lifelong fan of holiday camps, remembers, 'He took us on rambles, especially into the camp's private woodlands where he would give us lessons in natural history. Every day after lunch we would all go around to his chalet where he would entertain us with songs, stories, puppets and best of all, balloons.'

Below: Fancy Dress and Talent contests like this one at Skegness helped to keep the kids entertained.

It was the organised fun and entertainment that made the camps so popular and all with the assurance that the fun 'n' games would go on even in bad weather. The Butlin's catchphrase was 'When it's wet it's always fine at Butlin's.' In the 1950s and 60s every Butlin's camp boasted a resident revue company, two dance bands and an orchestra as well as the repertory company that performed popular plays cut down to sixty minutes. At a time when entertainment was not so readily available as it is today, the repertoire of shows, concerts and dancing was something out of the ordinary. Campers got to see top acts before television brought them to everyone's homes.

The timetable of communal activities was one of the keys to its success. There were morning exercises,

swimming galas, sports, competitions, ballroom dancing, cabarets, bingo, billiards, donkey derbys and all the games associated with school sports days from egg 'n' spoon to sack races. One of the most interesting aspects of the holiday camp was the way it encouraged the Brits to shake off their natural reserve, do the un-British thing and all join in together. This wasn't always the case. When Billy Butlin first opened Skegness, he noticed that something was missing. 'Many of the campers did not take advantage of the recreational facilities. Often they sat about aimlessly, keeping to their own family groups. Even more worrying was the fact that some of them looked bored! It became clear that we needed to involve them more in the life of the place. It was not enough to provide facilities, people had to be encouraged to use them.' What was needed was a way of getting the campers to mix, someone to break the ice and encourage people to join in – and so the Redcoat was born, to be followed by the Bluecoats at Pontin's and the Greencoats at Warner's. 'The joke was that the Redcoats forced you to enjoy yourself,' says Frank Stephens who holidayed in Ayr in the 1950s. 'If they saw a couple who were sitting there out of it, they'd go along to them and say, "Come along now, why aren't you dancing?" And one of the girls would grab hold of the man and dance with him and the boys would get hold of the lady and dance with her. They didn't actually force you but if you didn't want to take part you were encouraged to go along and support people in the competitions.'

The timetable of organised activities was relentless, the fun was never allowed to stop. It was like a continuous sports day with prizes for everyone. If you didn't like team spirit, then you were in the wrong place. Many joked that it was more like an army camp than a holiday centre. A great many of the holidaymakers, of course, had first-hand experience of army camps, National Service only having been phased out in May 1960. For Brenda Bullock, who visited Butlin's in the late 40s and 50s, they were all in it together. 'The camp was organised like a school, with the Redcoats to get us into order, and the whole of the campers were divided up into members of one of four houses. Just as in school, battles to the death took place in sporting contests between the houses.'

Above left: Three young Butlin's fans display a Butlin's towel . . . now was there a fight over who got to keep it?

Top: Typical Butlin's events programmes from 1956.

Above: 'Bill and Ben' was a popular children's TV programme and obviously inspired these young fancy dress competitors.

Weekly competitions organised by the uniformed staff proved to be a highly successful way of involving people and breaking the ice. The competitions catered for virtually everyone on the site from Knobbly Knees to Junior Miss, Holiday Princess, Ugly Face, Miss Lovely Legs, Glamorous Grandmother, Tarzan, Bonny Babies, Bathing Beauties, the Shiniest Bald Head, Happy Family and Fancy Dress. In the 1950s there were Princess Elizabeth and Marilyn Monroe lookalike competitions. Some of the competitions were sponsored, such as the Shaver of the Week by Philishave, makers of electric razors, Rizla sponsored the Cigarette Rolling competition and Lux sponsored one for the Loveliest Complexion. Marjorie Chalker recalls, 'I was an avid joiner-in. I was always game for anything and sometimes I could hear people groaning, "Not her again." I was always the first up for the 'Miss Lovely Legs' competition. I knew I had no chance of winning, my legs were like tree trunks, I just did it for a laugh. One year I entered the Fancy Hat competition, where you had to make a hat to represent a song title. I put two tins of baby food on my head and went as the can-can!'

The commercial genius of Butlin was that he devised a holiday in which, for the most part, the campers entertained each other, either as performers or as the audience. And it was all for free, thus keeping the costs down and making an attractive package. To provide an added incentive for camp competitions there were a host of prizes supplied free by advertisers and sponsors eager to plug their products. The star prize, 'a free holiday at the Butlin's camp of your choice' was another inspired sales gimmick, helping to keep down costs and fill up camps for

Top: Ballroom dancing competitions were a regular feature at Butlin's.

Above: Redcoats, there to entertain you . . .

the next year. The catch was that adults only won one free holiday – the rest of the family had to pay for themselves. 'My son won a free holiday and we all celebrated,' says Margaret Maudsley. 'Then it dawned on me that I'd have to pay for all the other kids to go to take up this free place. I wasn't going to do it but my son pestered and pestered me so we all eventually went. And in the end we had a lovely time.'

In the 1950s, Stuart Gillespie from Liverpool devised a cunning way to beat the system and win free holidays for all his family. 'I fancied myself as a bit of a stand-up comedian and I managed to win the variety competition several years running at different camps. That was one of the main reasons we went, it was a wonderful feeling to win and there was a real chance you might be discovered. I wasn't, but at least we had free holidays year after year. The problem was paying for my wife and my son. I cracked it by accident really. I'd trained up my son to tell jokes, I thought he might make a career out of it, so that at the age of six he was very funny. Well, he used to win the children's talent competition and as he was so young he got a free holiday for himself and his mother. So we all went for nothing, fantastic.'

By the 1950s and 60s the holiday camps were entering a golden era and had become the number one choice for millions of British holidaymakers. At their peak Butlin's nine camps were catering for 60,000 campers a week. With their mixture of daily outdoor activities, fully catered meals, serviced chalets and evening entertainment for an all-inclusive price they were the forerunners of the modern package holiday.

Top: Early morning physical jerks kept the campers young and beautiful.

Above: Smile! Bonny babies at Butlin's in Ayr in the 60s.

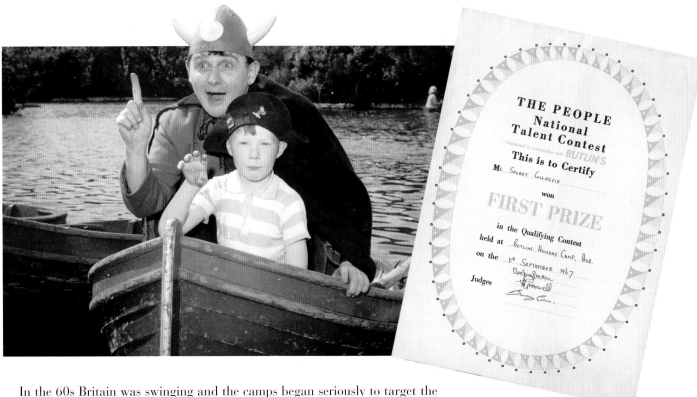

In the 60s Britain was swinging and the camps began seriously to target the modern younger generation. A new type of camper was catered for – the single teenager.

They had money and freedom to go on holiday without their parents. They headed for Butlin's and Pontin's on their scooters where there was free entertainment during the evening and free activities during the day. While at home there was often just the pub and a dance at the weekend to look forward to, the holiday camps offered rock'n'roll ballrooms, jukeboxes, coffee bars and special teenage chalets. In the early 1960s Butlin's in particular made a big effort to keep up with the latest teenage trends, constantly inviting the Pathé newsreel cameras to show they were providing facilities for every new craze from roller-skating to the twist – with best dancer competitions held by the poolside. During the summer months it wasn't unusual to find 3,000 single young people at one Butlin's camp in any one week.

Above: Stuart Gillespie and his son both won talent competitions as stand-up comedians.

Pete Bradshaw from Burnley was an apprentice painter and decorator when he went to Butlin's at Filey in 1962 with a group of other teenage friends. It was his first holiday away from his parents. 'There was no liberation at home, you couldn't take a girl back to your parents'. Going to Butlin's was a way to get away from that control, to have some fun.' Burnley's Wakes Week was at the start of July and on arrival he discovered that hundreds of other Burnley residents were at Butlin's, too.

During the day Pete and his mates eschewed the communal activities to hang out by the swimming pool. 'There were large indoor swimming pools which were unusual for the time; it was brilliant – everything seemed better than at home.' They organised football games against the Glasgow boys who had the same Wakes Week and when the alcohol was flowing, fights would break out between the Burnley and the Glasgow lads.

But the teenage campers soon gave Butlin's a bad name. Towards the middle

of the 60s gang fights started and teenagers began to vandalise some of the camps. On one night a hundred were evicted by security men from a single site. But even more damaging to its family image was its growing reputation as a hotbed of illicit sex. Rumours went around that sex-mad teenagers were holding orgies in the chalets. The sexual activity was supposedly not just among the campers. The Redcoats too had a reputation for the roving eye, picking out new sexual partners from each new intake. So great was their reputation for sexual prowess that they were immortalised in the *Confessions From . . .* series of books by Timothy Lea, who ranked them up there in the same league as window cleaners and driving instructors. In *Confessions From A Holiday Camp* the hero scores on almost every page as a Holiday Host at Melody Bay Holiday Camp. His mother sums it up succinctly by saying, 'Well, we all know what goes on at holiday camps, don't we?' The naughty goings-on were nothing new. Even in the 1930s there were rumours of loose morals in the camps. Newspaper articles appeared about 'painted ladies' (a period euphemism for prostitutes) mingling among the guests, although it is probable that many such stories were started by jealous hoteliers who were feeling the pinch.

Contemporary interviews from the 1960s with teenage campers do suggest that the pill and the more permissive sexual attitudes of the day did mean that Butlin's attracted teenagers on the lookout for casual sex. One of them was Mike McGregor from Dagenham in East London. 'I went to Pwllheli with my mates. We lied about

Above: The boys are back in town: Pete Bradshaw (far right) and his mates get the drinks in.

Below: Free activities during the day and free entertainment at night were big holiday camp attractions for unaccompanied teenagers.

our ages to get in, because they had an age restriction if you were unaccompanied. We said we were eighteen when we were only sixteen. The main attraction was the girls and we picked them out in the canteen, you'd get chatting together then you'd see them later at all the entertainments or invite them back to the chalets at night. We were such innocents, we didn't know what we were doing and my first experience of sex there was a bit of a disaster. It seemed to me it was the girls who were much more experienced, they were away from home for a week, no restrictions at all, and they knew what they wanted.'

Above: Mike McGregor, in sunglasses, and his friends play it cool.

The reality of teenage sex life in the camps was, however, far less sensational than it was portayed in the popular press. Pete Bradshaw's experiences in the early 60s were typical of many: 'We'd be out drinking every evening and go to listen to the dance bands which was where I got to know the girls. Then I'd try and get one back to the chalet before the others rolled in at closing time. But I never really got beyond a kiss and a cuddle before the others got back.'

Some of the female members of staff who showed a strong interest in the young male campers often had a very traditional ulterior motive – they were looking for an eligible young man to wed. Ann Preen worked as a waitress during the summer season at Butlin's in Clacton in 1960, 1962 and 1964. 'There were lots of Irish girls who came to work in Butlin's, a lot of them were on the lookout for a nice English man to marry.' Ann met Colin during the 1964 season. 'He had recently separated from his wife and was on a break. I didn't normally associate with men who'd been married before but I fell in love with him. For Colin it was also love at first sight. He went hoping for a good time but ended up with me!'

Below: The same can't be said of this lot.

But as the bad publicity continued, in the late 60s Butlin's took action to limit the damage. Teenage sleeping quarters were segregated from families and they were also penned into their own section of the dining hall. In some camps they were given their own chalet

lines at the far end of the site with boys in one row and girls in another, both regularly patrolled by security men. Chalet patrols were spending as much time checking that people of the right sex were sleeping in the right cabins as they were listening out for crying babies. Families were by now being put off the holiday camps by the rowdy and 'sexually permissive' young people and in 1968 Butlin's stopped group bookings from single teenagers and tried to re-brand the camps, stressing their family image. Pontin's and Warner's quickly followed suit.

Even more damaging to the popularity of holiday camps was their reputation for regimentation. This had been a common criticism since the early days. The recently demobbed Arthur Barwick who went to Butlin's in 1946 recalls, 'I couldn't stand the wakey-wakey calls in the morning. At 7.30 the blowers would be going, "Breakfast is ready!" It was like being back in the army, all that was missing was the bugle.'

Stuart Gillespie from Liverpool, who went to Pwllheli in the 1950s and 60s, remembers, 'All the chalets had speakers cemented to the walls and you couldn't

Left: 'Anyone for tea?' Ann Preen (far right) on duty in the early 1960s.

switch the damned things off. I tried to put the pillow over mine. If you were on a second sitting for breakfast, you didn't want to know it was time for the first sitting people to get up.'

Brenda Bullock, who grew up on a council estate in Birmingham in the 1950s, recalls, 'It never entered our heads that we shouldn't be ordered about. Being working class we were all used to being regimented and didn't flinch when at some unearthly hour some hideously cheerful voice came over the tannoy wishing us "Good Morning Campers." But by the 60s this old deference was wearing thin, as was the camaraderie spawned by the war. Some of the antics of the Redcoats to get everyone to join in were increasingly seen as bullying and an intrusion of individual privacy and freedom.

One of their victims was Mary Greenhough, who holidayed at Butlin's Filey camp. 'Over the tannoy came the announcement that our day would start down

at the pool. A Redcoat was already down there ready to lead us off to some activity. There was a few of us sitting around the pool anyway and there were these Redcoats coming around and they were getting hold of people and hanging them over the railings and passing them down to a Redcoat at the bottom and then he'd throw them into the swimming pool. Well, I was terrified because I didn't like water and I couldn't swim so I climbed up higher, so they couldn't get us and my friend did the same. We never went back to the swimming pool and I thought, "Well, if that's Butlin's I'm not going any more," and I never have.'

By the late 60s holidaymakers were starting to lose the holiday camp habit. The social and sexual revolutions had changed attitudes to everything including what people wanted from a holiday – and the holiday camp was not it. Tastes were becoming more sophisticated, people were looking for new experiences and more holidaymakers were beginning to travel abroad.

It was really the boom in package holidays abroad that dealt the worst blow to the holiday camp. Campers were escaping *en masse* over the security fence to the Costa Brava where a week in the sun could be had for a few hundred pounds. The prospect of a holiday with sunshine guaranteed was more tempting than a holiday in Britain with the likelihood of rain. Both Butlin's and Pontin's responded with their own overseas ventures. Butlin's tried a camp in the Bahamas and Pontin's 'went Pontinental' opening holiday camps in Sardinia, Torremolinos and Majorca. Marjorie Chalker went to the Pontinental in Majorca in 1967 for her first trip abroad. She was on her own. 'I'd been to Pontin's before and trusted them. I thought it was a safe way of going abroad, I knew there'd be lots of English people there, I wouldn't have tried anything else. I wasn't very

Above: Marjorie Chalker posing outside her Pontinental chalet in Majorca, 1967.

Top: Fun in the sun tempted people away from British holiday camps.

adventurous and only had a few words of Spanish. We arrived at the resort in the dark, I felt really frightened and went to the bar. I didn't know what to drink so I ordered a vodka, even though I'd never drunk vodka before. I went back to the chalet and cried, thinking I'd made a horrible mistake. But the next day when I woke up the sun came out, I could hear glorious little birds and smell the pine forest, I knew it was all going to be fine.'

Despite their appeal for holiday camp devotees and the more cautious continental traveller, neither Pontinental nor Butlin's overseas survived for long. The British were acquiring more adventurous tastes beyond that of an old-style British holiday camp set in sunnier climes. In contrast the French equivalent, Club Med, has thrived and grown to be one of the largest holiday companies in the world. Club Med took French holidaymakers to the shores of the Mediterranean where guests played at desert islands, living close to nature in simple Polynesian straw huts and using beads for money. The role of the *gentils organisateurs*, the equivalent of the Redcoats, was much more laid-back; there were fewer allusions to the prison camp and more to getting close to a simple, natural life. Such was the appeal of Club Med it soon overtook Butlin's and Pontin's in attracting thousands of young British holidaymakers to holiday camps abroad.

Top: Sub-tropical swimming paradise at Center Parcs, Sherwood Forest.

Above: Tropical paradise Club Med style in Bora Bora

By the late 1970s many of the camps at home were looking weather-beaten and worn, and the public's appetite for communal hijinks was fading fast. A change of image was called for. The camps underwent a makeover to bring them up to date. Self-catering chalets were introduced so that 'guests' as they became known (the word 'camper' was banned) could have more independence. The word 'dinner' was taken off the evening menu at Butlin's because a lot of campers had 'dinner' at midday. To avoid the jokes about Colditz the sites were no longer called camps but refashioned as holiday centres, villages or parks instead. The reputation for over-regimentation was tackled, too. The regular tannoy announcements to happy campers were toned down and the last

wakey-wakey call was made in 1979. When Bobby Butlin took over from his father Billy he introduced the slogan 'Butlin's Land is Freedom Land' to emphasise the independence of the guests. For a while Butlin's even abandoned its name in an attempt to escape its *Hi-de-Hi* past. Bognor Regis was relaunched as Southcoast World and Minehead became Somerwest World, both after major investment and refurbishment. By the early 1980s the camps were in financial crisis and Butlin's was forced to close its two camps at Clacton and Filey. This was the beginning of a series of closures which left only three Butlin's camps in the UK by the end of the 1980s – at Skegness, Blackpool and Minehead.

There was new competition on the home front too. In the late 80s Center Parcs introduced the continental concept of holiday parks with villas set in natural woodland. Their slogan was, 'We wouldn't dream of organising you.' In locations like Sherwood Forest in Nottinghamshire, the new rival offered family fun in the sun – and the rain – thanks to a gigantic dome that could turn a slice of the Midlands into a fair approximation of Majorca. The journalist David Aaronovitch described a holiday at Longleat Center Parcs in 1998 as being 'an arboreal Butlin's for men and women of taste'. The middle classes who, pre-parenthood, were enjoying the sensual delights of cappuccino in sunbaked Tuscan

Top: Butlin's indoor pools were a great attraction when first introduced.

Above: Non-swimmer Mary Greenhough was horrified when Redcoats threw guests in the pool.

villages were, post-parenthood, holidaying in an upmarket, new-wave holiday camp with activities to occupy the children. For parents on a health kick there were seaweed wraps in the 'Aqua Sauna' club – and for those looking to indulge themselves there was the *chocolatier*.

The two great names of the holiday camp – Butlin's and Pontin's – continue today but on a much smaller scale. They have updated themselves and diversified by introducing elements of the theme park like waterworlds and funfair rides and by offering specialist activities like salsa and rock'n'roll weekends. But essentially their appeal is still to families looking for a safe holiday at home with activities for the children. The legacy of the holiday camp survives though. Forerunners of the package holiday, they helped to pioneer more child-friendly, communal and entertaining holidays than ever before. They also brought people together to socialise in a way they never would have done before. As Frank Stephens, a Butlin's holidaymaker of the post-war years recalls, 'As soon as you got through the gates you threw off your suit and tie, put on your camp shirt and you felt you were the same as everyone else.'

In their heyday in the late 1940s and 50s the camps had marked the end of each day with a sing-song – 30 years later it would become their swansong.

> *Goodnight Campers, I can see you yawning*
> *Goodnight Campers, see you in the morning*
> *You must cheer up or you'll soon be dead*
> *For I've heard it said, folks die in bed*
> *So we'll say good-night, Campers, don't sleep in your braces*
> *Goodnight Campers, put your teeth in Jeye's*
> *Drown your sorrow, bring the bottles back tomorrow*
> *Goodnight Campers Goodnight.*

Left: In the heyday of the holiday camp in the late 40s this booking agent devoted only a fraction of its window display to Cook's Tours (bottom left) - the rest was reserved for Butlin's.

HOLIDAYS ON A SHOESTRING

'If you didn't have the money for a holiday, the next best thing was hop-picking. For people like me who lived in the docks it was fantastic to get out of the smokey atmosphere, to camp in a little hut in the countryside and see foxes and rabbits running across the fields.'

Above: Camping gave many of the poorer city dwellers their first real taste of the countryside.

Eastender Stan Little was one of millions of poorer city dwellers who, after World War II, couldn't afford a proper holiday but desperately wanted to get away for a break. Other than an occasional awayday to the coast by coach or train, they had two main choices. They could sign up for a working agricultural holiday such as hop-picking or take one of the cheapest and most affordable holidays of all – camping. In the 1950s and 60s they didn't just stay in tents. They also bedded down in an extraordinary variety of disused buses, trams, railway coaches, cabins, huts and derelict farm buildings, all of which were brought out of retirement to house campers on a shoestring budget.

From the late 19th century onwards, camping grew in popularity as a means of escaping from the smokey, disease-ridden industrial cities and living, at least for a week or two, close to nature. For some idealists and utopian socialists it even represented a romantic return to a simple life on the land. The main devotees of camping in Edwardian Britain, however, were the politically conservative, uniformed youth movements. It was the Boy's Brigade and subsequently the Boy Scouts and Girl Guides that brought the experience of organised camping to millions of children. Robert Baden-Powell held his first camp at Brownsea Island in Dorset in 1907 where he put into practice his ideas for training young people for responsible citizenship and taught them skills like pitching tents, using maps and compasses and cooking over a wood fire. Scouting immediately caught on, with one of the key attractions being the camps. At one of the first rallies held at Crystal Palace in September 1909, over 11,000 scouts attended. It was all inspired by the Boer War and was regarded by Baden-Powell as a palatable way of instilling army discipline and moral fibre in the nation's youth. But it was in fact the coming of World War I in 1914 that brought the experience of camping to the widest public. Many soldiers who had experienced life under canvas in bell tents missed the sing-songs, the shared experience and the sense of camaraderie which had helped them survive the horrors of trench warfare. They continued camping for fun when the war was over.

During the 1920s and 30s camping in Britain became less nationalistic and militaristic. Although the Scouts and Guides remained sex-segregated, alternative youth movements like the Woodcraft Folk, set up for the children of the labour movement, pioneered mixed camps and by the 1930s had several thousand members. Camping was also promoted by the inter-war health and beauty movement which

Opposite top: The 3rd Westcliff Scout Troop, having just returned from summer camp in 1913.

Opposite right and middle: With their church connections and healthy outdoor pursuits, organisations like the Boy's Brigade and the Scout movement were seen to be character forming for youngsters.

Opposite bottom: Scouts gather at a vast camp in Sutton Coldfield, near Birmingham, to celebrate the centenary of Baden-Powell's birthday in 1957.

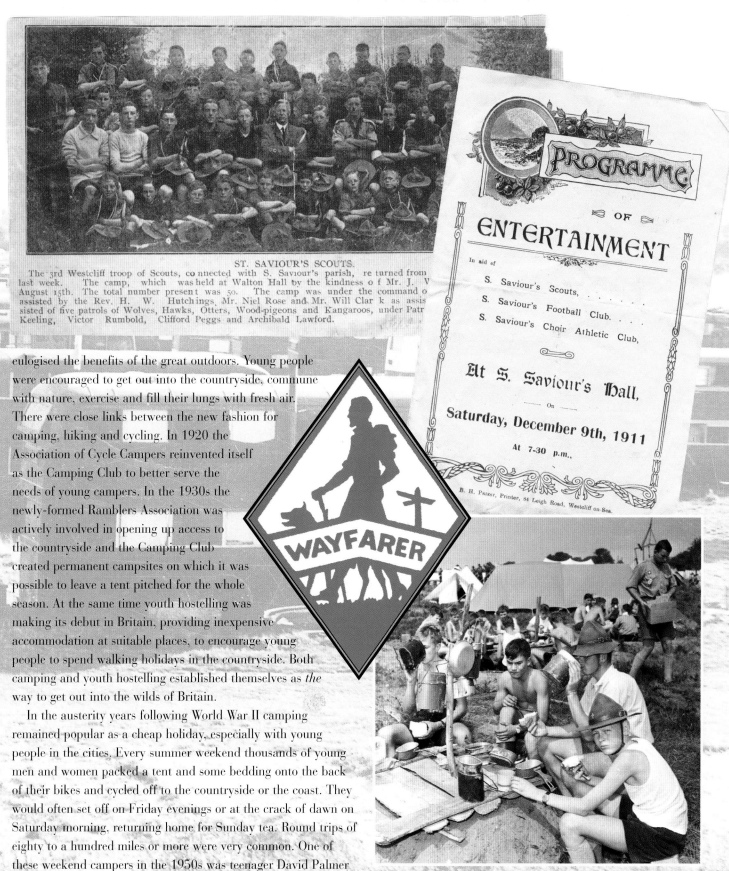

ST. SAVIOUR'S SCOUTS.

The 3rd Westcliff troop of Scouts, connected with S. Saviour's parish, returned from last week. The camp, which was held at Walton Hall by the kindness of Mr. J. V August 15th. The total number present was 50. The camp was under the command o assisted by the Rev. H. W. Hutchings, Mr. Niel Rose and Mr. Will Clark as assis sisted of five patrols of Wolves, Hawks, Otters, Wood-pigeons and Kangaroos, under Patr Keeling, Victor Rumbold, Clifford Peggs and Archibald Lawford.

PROGRAMME

OF

ENTERTAINMENT

In aid of

S. Saviour's Scouts,

S. Saviour's Football Club. . . .

S. Saviour's Choir Athletic Club,

At S. Saviour's Hall,

On

Saturday, December 9th, 1911

At 7-30 p.m.,

B. H. Priest, Printer, 84 Leigh Road, Westcliff on Sea.

WAYFARER

eulogised the benefits of the great outdoors. Young people were encouraged to get out into the countryside, commune with nature, exercise and fill their lungs with fresh air. There were close links between the new fashion for camping, hiking and cycling. In 1920 the Association of Cycle Campers reinvented itself as the Camping Club to better serve the needs of young campers. In the 1930s the newly-formed Ramblers Association was actively involved in opening up access to the countryside and the Camping Club created permanent campsites on which it was possible to leave a tent pitched for the whole season. At the same time youth hostelling was making its debut in Britain, providing inexpensive accommodation at suitable places, to encourage young people to spend walking holidays in the countryside. Both camping and youth hostelling established themselves as *the* way to get out into the wilds of Britain.

In the austerity years following World War II camping remained popular as a cheap holiday, especially with young people in the cities. Every summer weekend thousands of young men and women packed a tent and some bedding onto the back of their bikes and cycled off to the countryside or the coast. They would often set off on Friday evenings or at the crack of dawn on Saturday morning, returning home for Sunday tea. Round trips of eighty to a hundred miles or more were very common. One of these weekend campers in the 1950s was teenager David Palmer

Holidays On A Shoestring

from Colne in Lancashire.

'Me and my friends, we couldn't ever afford to go off for Wakes Weeks holidays, money was still that tight. We couldn't even afford to go for the day in a coach or by train. So, if the weather was good, we used to cycle to Blackpool every weekend in the summer. We'd pack the little tent, I'd pinch my mum's patchwork quilt, ground sheet, Primus stove, it'd all be on the bikes, then we'd set off. It was a good 35 miles. That'd take us about four hours. No problem, we were used to it. Then we'd set up the tent on the dunes near South Street station. There'd be several tents pitched up there, it was against the rules; the railway owned it and inspectors would come and threaten you, but they never took any action. We said we'd go, then they went away and we just put the tent up behind the next dune. It was a wonderful spot, the tide never came in that far and you were well placed for all the entertainments next morning.

'We'd cook up bacon and egg that we'd take with us first thing in the morning, then off to the toilets opposite Madame Tussaud's for a wash and brush up. There were loads of lads there doing the same as us, some had just slept in sleeping bags on the beach or under the pier. Then we'd get our kiss-me-quick hat out and stroll down the prom. If any girls looked happy we'd give them a kiss and a cuddle. The main aim was to get one back to the tent. It was only a tiny two-man tent so if you got lucky it was a bit crowded but we took it in turns, and one would go back early then another later.'

During the post-war years, camping also took off as an affordable

Above and below: The motorcycle and sidecar combination proved the ideal way for Ed Mitchell to take his family on a camping holiday.

56

family holiday. Its great advantage was that it cost next to nothing and could be organised independently without observing the petty regulations of a boarding house.

'Our camping holidays were very important because we hadn't a holiday before the war,' says Ed Mitchell, a bank messenger from Norwich. He took his family on camping holidays in the late 40s and 50s. 'I was determined that when I got out of the army I should have some holidays with my children, I had two by then. I bought some tents because we couldn't afford to do anything else. We didn't have the money to go to hotels and boarding houses but once you had the camping gear and paid for food and petrol, you had no further expense. It was a cheap holiday and a nice one, too, if the weather was decent.'

The massive growth in motor transport gave a big boost to camping holidays, providing easy access for families getting away from it all. In the early post-war years, however, a considerable number of families arrived by motorcycle or by coach – many attracted by this type of holiday couldn't afford cars. This didn't limit their ambition in planning trips to faraway campsites and many embarked on epic journeys across Britain. In the pre-motorway age of slow, winding country roads and low speeds, these trips could take several days. Camping on the way was part of the holiday. Ed Mitchell thought nothing of a four day journey. 'I bought a motorbike and sidecar to fit all the family in and set off from Norwich for Sandy Bay near Exmouth in Devon. It took a full four days to get down there. With a motorbike and sidecar you couldn't do more than about 35 to 40 miles an hour. I rode the motorbike. My son Graham, who was about seven years old, sat on the pillion at the back. Peggy, my wife, was in the sidecar but it used to make her bottom ache because the seat was just a bit of sponge covered over with leatherette. My daughter was behind her. We camped on the way down; we'd plan the holiday with a camping site book. On that trip I remember the first night was at Whipsnade Zoo, the second we got down just north of Bournemouth. It was all part of the holiday, stopping on the way, and it was a pleasure really to sit on the old motorbike, hear the engine throbbing underneath your legs and look at the countryside.'

Above: A group of female ramblers enjoying the countryside in Cumbria in 1960.

Derek Johnson from Glasgow remembers one family camping trip that turned into a holiday from hell. 'It was 1964 and a lot of my dad's friends were going to a campsite in Newquay in Cornwall for their holidays. So Dad decided that that was the very thing for us, too. The fact that we didn't have a car didn't bother him at all; he decided that we were going to travel down by bus – 28 hours on a bus down to

Holidays On A Shoestring

Newquay. We'd never been camping before but Dad bought lots of equipment which he'd seen advertised as "everything the family of four needed for the perfect camping holiday." We got to the bus station an hour early because he always liked to allow for disasters. Beside us were three giant bags, the tent, the camping equipment and a huge bag of food with tins of everything – soup, beans, dog meat. [Yes, the dog went as well!] The bus driver stopped dead in his tracks and said, "What the hell is all that?" He said we'd have to wait until all the other passengers got on to see if there was enough space to get all our luggage on.

'Eventually, we all got on with the bags around us for the 28-hour trip. Now my dad hadn't taken into account that I used to get terribly travel-sick – and so did the dog. So my mum gave me a travel sickness pill and had some tablets from the vet to calm the dog down. But I didn't really get on with travel sickness pills; they made me feel sick. The only way I could make a half decent journey was to lie flat out on the seat of the bus. My poor mum had to sit at the window with my head in her lap, me stretched out and my legs dangling over the edge. My mum had a carrier bag full of newspapers which she spread out on the floor and said, "If you're going to be sick, do it on that." I thought, great, now you're reminding me that I'm going to be sick. It wasn't one of these luxury coaches with air-conditioning, either, it was a basic single decker, an old rackety, bouncing bus. If it got too hot, the driver opened the door and let in a 30 mile-an-hour blast of wind.

'I remember at one point we'd stopped for a bite to eat. My dad asked how I was feeling and when I told him I was feeling a wee bit sick he threw another couple of pills down my throat. A bit later I was lying there and the bus was bouncing around and suddenly I felt peculiar and threw up. I was violently sick in the bus, all down my poor mum's leg. I managed to get most of it onto the paper and she had this towel and was wiping my face.

'People were craning their necks to see what was going on and my mum said, "He's just got a wee tummy upset." And while I'm lying there groaning, the dog's being sick, too, and my dad is sort of shoving newspapers under the dog's head so that it would land on the paper. This went on for the whole 28 hours. By the time we got to Cornwall I was completely spaced out, exhausted, dehydrated and starving because I hadn't been able to eat anything, and so was the dog, too. It was without a doubt the worst journey of my life, but once we'd pitched our tent, the sun came out, there was a nice breeze coming off the sea and we went into Newquay for some fish 'n' chips, I thought maybe this is going to be worth it after all.'

One characteristic feature of the British family camping holiday was the desire to create a real home-from-home by taking everything but the kitchen sink. For large families this sometimes meant a van or lorry needed to be hired to carry everything to the campsite.

Below: Two youngsters catch up on their reading at a summer camp run by the National Association for Gifted Children in 1967.

Above: Derek Johnson with his parents and his dog, having survived the coach trip from hell. The camping holiday itself turned out to be just as dire.

Irene Byrne from Bristol had six children when she decided to go on holiday for the first time in 1959. 'As well as the six we also fostered another two children, so we were in need of a break. My husband was a scoutmaster and knew a bit about camping so we decided to go to Brean Down in Somerset. We hired a removal van to take us down. Into it we packed the baby's cot, pushchair, a chest of drawers full of our clothes, the kitchen table, chairs, camp beds, trunks, paraffin stove, bowls, crockery, cutlery, pots and pans, blankets and an old surplus carpet, etc.'

It turned into an idyllic experience for the city dwellers, even though they were only forty miles from home. 'The children were enthralled; they'd never really seen cows before. The farmer would give us milk and the butcher, greengrocer, baker and ice-cream van stopped regularly on their way to deliver to the farms. We rose with the sun and went to bed when it got dark. We cooked on a barbecue, the children were free to play where they liked and for me it was a break from all the housework. We really got to know our children on that holiday and they each other.'

The perennial attraction of a camping holiday was the rare opportunity to sample the delights of country life and the wonders of nature. But being in the countryside wasn't without its own hazards. The discomforts ranged from muddy fields to mosquito bites and from sleepless nights on hard ground to the terrors of discovering that you were pitched next to a much larger animal.

Ed Mitchell remembers one close encounter at a campsite on the Isle of Wight. 'We'd pitched the tent and had settled down to sleep for the night. Early in the morning Peggy, my wife, woke me up saying there was someone outside. Sure enough, I could hear some heavy breathing going on outside the tent. So I got up to investigate, stepped over the children, undid the tent flaps to see what was going on.

As camping equipment became more sophisticated and affordable, everyday chores became less of an ordeal.

'There were these three red bullocks cropping the grass between the guy ropes. So, of course, I went up to them as though I was going to shoo them away, but they didn't move. They looked at me with their eyes and I thought hellfire, I hope they're not going to charge me. I grabbed a branch to defend myself, but just then the lady who ran the camp restaurant arrived on her bike. I said, "You've got to help me here. I've got a wife and children and we're trapped! They'll chomp on my ropes and have my tent down." She said the bullocks were from the monastery next door and they'd broken in before. So she went off to phone the monks and soon there was a monk running across the fields. He looked like he had a big brown dressing gown on. He had one of them habits and a funny haircut. He had

HOLIDAYS ON A SHOESTRING

a pail underneath his arm and started to rattle cow cake in there and he was shouting, "Come on, my darlings." Well, it was like a hen and chickens the way they responded and me, the wife and the kids were saved.'

The unpredictable British climate meant that the most common hazard facing the hapless camper was, of course, the rain. Bad weather and poor waterproofing blighted many a camping holiday. For Derek Johnson who had endured a terrible journey to get to a campsite in Cornwall in the 60s, the rain turned a bad experience into a washout. 'Once we'd settled in after the horrendous journey, we went to sleep. During the night it started to rain but not like a shower, it was a torrential downpour. And then it didn't stop, it went on for a full six days, non-stop constant rain bouncing off the tent. We had a full fortnight to wait for the bus to take us back home to Glasgow, so we were stuck. The tent itself was soaking – everything inside was starting to go damp, in that musty way. My poor mother had to cook three meals a day in that tent and we were

Below: Camping coaches had a special appeal for rail enthusiasts.

spending the night in damp sleeping bags. Well, what with the rain, the journey and the damp atmosphere, I developed a chest infection and was taken to the doctor's. But that wasn't much good because I could hardly get better sleeping in a damp tent, so my dad had to take me into Newquay to see the local minister and ask if he would let me sleep in one of the church pews. That was the worst holiday we ever had but the amazing thing was we carried on going down to Newquay for camping holidays and we had some very happy times.'

British campers were renowned for a certain stoicism, a determination to have a good time no matter how wet they got. Ed Mitchell always kept the fun 'n' games up. 'If it was raining we used to play Ludo in the tent and have a sing-song like *Ten Green Bottles*. We'd even go down to the beach to swim with a mac on over our swimming costumes. My wife would come down there with a couple of army groundsheets and put our clothes underneath to stay dry. We used to change on the beach in the rain and wipe off with a towel.'

Another form of camping, and one which had a special appeal for the railway enthusiast, was in 'camping coaches' converted from disused railway carriages. Led by the London & North Eastern Railway, which pioneered the idea in the 1930s, former passenger coaches were kitted out with sleeping accommodation, kitchens and living areas, then placed in country station sidings where the public hired them for a week or two as holiday homes during the summer season. This novel idea of 'camping coach holidays' was so successful that by the 1950s the scheme was in place all over the country and run by British Railways. They were advertised as 'a cheap and ideal holiday for the family' providing an 'out-of-doors camping holiday with the comfort of well-appointed living accommodation at reasonable cost.' Most of the camping coaches were sited near the coast and families booked in at picturesque stations like Dawlish Warren and Barmouth, some on remote branches with only a few trains passing

through each day, but others on busy main lines.

Des Cox from Derbyshire spent his teenage holidays in the mid-1950s in a camping coach at Abergele station in North Wales. 'My Dad worked on the railways so he was entitled to cheap holidays in the camping coaches and free rail travel. There were lots of other railway workers' families, too. I remember being woken very early every morning by the Irish mail train blowing its whistle as it passed through the station! Then the first thing I'd do was to open the window by pulling down the leather strap so that I could hear the sea on the pebbles. It was wonderful.'

The Hornby family (no pun intended) of Bury, Lancashire, spent many a happy holiday in camping coaches on the Welsh coast around Talsarnau during the 1950s. 'There were about 12 to 14 of us who would go and we were really excited about it especially as we were young and hadn't had a family holiday ever before,' recalls Margaret Hornby, a teenager in the 1950s. 'We were a large family and it was the type

Above: The Hornby family enjoyed the togetherness of a camping coach holiday.

Holidays On A Shoestring

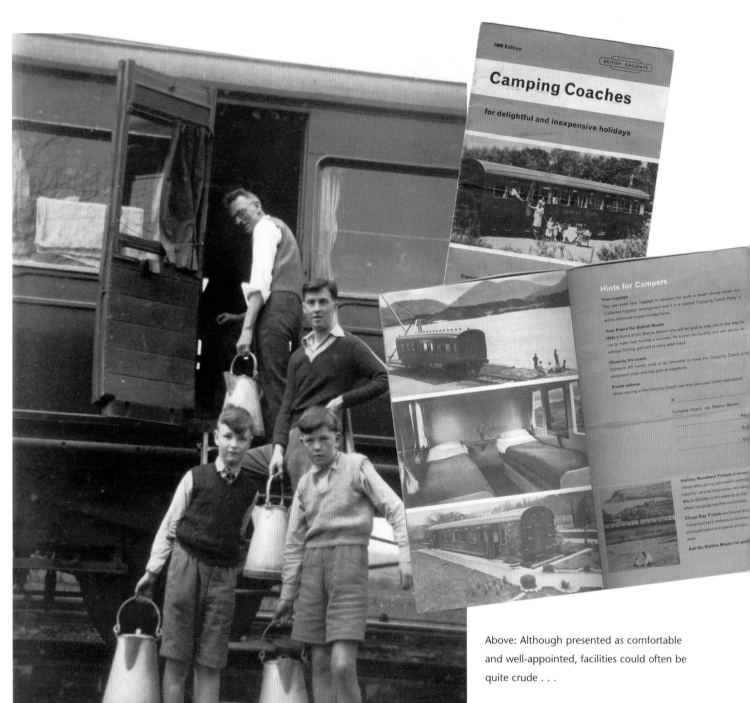

Above: Although presented as comfortable and well-appointed, facilities could often be quite crude . . .

Left: . . . here the Hornby family collect their water supplies.

of holiday where we could all go together and enjoy the same things. There was always several generations there from Auntie Elsie in her 60s down to our niece who was just a child. When we arrived at the station you only had to walk a few more yards to a siding to get to the camping coach. They were really basic railway carriages from the outside. Inside half of the coach was the living quarters where the kitchen, big table and chairs would be. The corridor led into where the bedrooms were, there were just plain ordinary bunk beds with a curtain across the doorway. It was pretty basic; there was no running water, we had to carry it from the railway station and we had a key to get into the station toilet. There was no electricity, just an oil-fired cooker and lights. It was never quite bright enough to read at night, so we would sit in bed and read under the blanket with a torch.'

Margaret's niece, Rosemary Timms, was impressed by the courtesy of the station staff who looked after them. 'The station master was a Mr Hughes and he was always there to greet us. When we arrived he'd arrange for a box of groceries to be waiting in the kitchen, which included treats we wouldn't normally get at home – like Puffed Wheat! The coach overlooked the sea which was lovely. There was a lot of freedom and fresh air. I always think of them as being proper holidays, just the job for us coming from industrial Lancashire.'

For the many children and grown ups who shared the very British love for steam trains, there were some distinct advantages in having holidays on rails. Enid Hornby remembers, 'Every evening the Royal Mail train would stop and it was lovely to be able to post your postcards right into the train there on the station. During the day we used to sit on the platform and wait for the trains to go past and wave to all the passengers.'

The station master was the genial host, the equivalent of the seaside landlady. 'It was just a tiny branch line so we were lucky to have the station master all to ourselves. He'd tell us about the best walks in the area and give us information about trains to other places. He'd even ring through to all the other station masters up the line to tell them we were

Above: Rows of double decker buses – cheap camping accommodation in the 1940s and 50s.

on the way. We got friendly with the drivers, too, and by the end of the week we'd be allowed to chat to them when they stopped at the station. It was the best kind of holiday you could have, better than a tent, better than a caravan, because we were with just our family, on a branch line away from everybody else, near the mountains of Wales and the sea.'

The railway carriages on branch lines had a romantic appeal but many thousands of old, discarded wooden railway carriages, some built in the Victorian era, were brought out of retirement to provide the cheapest accommodation on campsites. With little or no refurbishment they generally formed the lowest end of the self-catering holiday market – though to disguise their true identity they were sometimes described as 'log cabins.'

In 1956 Edna Thomas of Fareham in Hampshire booked a fantastically cheap holiday for less than a pound in one such 'log cabin' on the Isle of Wight. 'At the time, we wondered what the catch was, but money was tight, we had two young children and couldn't afford much. When we got there we discovered what these log cabins really were – they were cranky old railway carriages. We had to sleep on the bench

HOLIDAYS ON A SHOESTRING

Above: The Marsden Family in front of their bus in Bridlington.

seats and store our belongings in the luggage racks above our heads. It poured with rain, the carriages leaked, the pillows had ticks on them, everything was covered in dirt and we all got ill. After three nights we gave up and went home. Of course, my son went and told all his schoolfriends that we'd spent the holiday in a dirty old railway carriage."

Many of the early post-war campsites evolved into caravan sites, fitting vans in alongside the tents. Although caravans were becoming increasingly popular as a more sophisticated version of camping, there were insufficient caravans to meet the demand, and many an aspiring entrepreneur was busy improvising an alternative. Ancient buses and trams built in the first decades of the century were saved from the scrapyard and given a new lease of life as holiday homes. One of the larger sites offering old, converted double-deckers to let was in Bridlington. The site was especially popular with Yorkshire miners looking for a cheap week away from their pit villages.

Alan Marsden used to holiday there with three generations of his family in the late 1940s and 50s. 'We waited all year for our week's holiday. It was the highlight of the year. It was the only time you saw your relations – aunties and uncles and cousins – apart from Christmas. We'd rent a couple of buses next to each other so that we'd all fit in. The buses had all the seats removed. Upstairs were the bedrooms, partitioned off. Downstairs was the lounge and living area. Where the driver's seat had been was where the coal was kept, behind the driver was the range for cooking and in the side sections were the dining room and chairs. Where the conductor kept his tickets was the larder. There was nothing posh about it, it had all been done on the cheap side but it

64

was good. There was no gas or electricity and the lighting was paraffin lamps, we had to bring the water in in buckets. Every night it was infested with bugs and we had great fun going on bug hunts with candles in the bus.'

'We had to do a lot of walking because the camp was about two miles away from the beach and we'd walk back at dinner times as well before going down to the beach again. In the evenings we played cards or dominoes or did a jigsaw in the buses. I think my father chose the double-decker holiday because it was cheap. We didn't have a lot of money in them days; he was a miner and wasn't on good money and it was a way of having a holiday at a time when few people from our village had a chance of going away. So we were lucky to go in these old buses, even though it was pretty primitive and a bit rough at times.'

An alternative kind of cheap camping holiday, very popular in the years immediately after World War II, was the working holiday on the land. Many farms experienced a shortage of labour after the war and to address this need in 1946 the Ministry of Agriculture campaigned with the slogan 'Lend a Hand on the Land' to promote the idea of working holidays on farms during the fruit, cereal and potato harvests. One of those who answered the call was Pat Withers, then just 18 and working in the Post Office in Birmingham. She was living with her grandmother at the time but wanted to go on holiday with a friend. 'Because the "Lend a Hand on the Land" scheme was run by the Ministry of Agriculture, my grandmother thought it would be a safe, supervised thing for young girls to do, "a very laudable activity." We

Top: hop-picking on Whitbread's Farm in Kent.

Above: Lola Smith and her family on a hop-picking holiday.

went down to Worcestershire and worked on a farm picking fruit and digging potatoes. It was back-breaking work and we fell into bed every night aching and moaning like mad, but there was a tremendous spirit. There was a really good mix of people; we met all sorts, some French lads, boys from Yorkshire, intellectuals from Oxford. I remember particularly a young Jewish woman of about 30 who'd had a rotten war. That was one of the biggest attractions, meeting people outside your normal social circle – oh, and it was a great way to meet the opposite sex.'

In the late 1940s Ray Rochford, a building worker from Salford, went potato picking in Cheshire. 'We'd pick the spuds, top 'n' tail the beets, pick the swedes, too. It was hard work but, by God, you were as fit as a butcher's dog when you were finished. You were tanned and muscular, which went down well with the country girls.'

For Ray, a working holiday was a welcome escape from the polluted atmosphere of the city. 'It was a wonderful holiday away from stinking Salford, far away from all those fumes and dingy streets. The first time we went, we got onto the Cheshire Plains and stood there looking at the panoramic view. I could smell this really lovely sweet smell and I said to Joe, "What's that?" I thought it was maybe the soapworks in the distance, you know, back in Salford. It was the hollyhocks and the roses and I thought, "What a beautiful place this must be to live, I'm really going to enjoy this fortnight." And I did. I was struck by how you could hear voices two or three fields away and birds singing. What a relief it was to get away from Salford and actually work under those conditions – you didn't want the money, although you did get paid, and they fed you too – pork and beef – and rationing was still on at the time. It was great just being there and savouring a different life altogether. I'd never imagined life in the countryside.'

The most popular of all the working holidays was hop-picking. There were hop-pickers in a number of industrial cities: every autumn many poor Birmingham families flocked to the hopfields of Herefordshire. But the largest exodus of all was the migration of Eastenders to the hop fields of Kent. The annual trip to the Kentish gardens to harvest hops for beer was a long tradition in many families and the British equivalent of the

Above: Stan Little and son hop-picking in the late 1940s.

Below: Whitbread-sponsored entertainment for the hop-pickers – drinking a yard of ale.

French *rendanges*, the seasonal grape picking for wine. By the turn of the 20th century, East Londoners had become the main source of casual labour used by Kent farmers during the hop harvest. At its peak, around a quarter of a million people made the trip from London to go 'down hopping.' 'Hoppers' specials' trains ran in season from London to Kent up until 1960, but many only treated themselves to the rail fare on the way back when they had the money in their pockets. Lola Smith from Bethnal Green, now in her 60s, remembers how most families would travel down on the backs of lorries carrying everything they needed for their stay. As soon as they crossed over Tower Bridge they began singing the age old hopping songs.

When you get down hopping, hopping down in Kent, you only went down hopping, to earn the bloody rent. The farmer calls us slackers, slackers we may be, but if it wasn't for us hoppers, where would the farmer be?

The season was quite short, usually a few weeks in September and October, but it gave many hard-up Cockneys the opportunity to get out into the countryside, earn some money, have a bit of a holiday and enjoy some autumn sun. 'I spent the best years of my life hopping.' says Lola Smith. 'To get into that country, it was magic, you were in another world. I mean, we'd come out of a narrow little terraced house district, fog, horrible, all the houses crammed in, so to get out to the country, white gates to the farm, trees, ditches, hay fields . . . whenever we saw a haystack, we'd go berserk jumping off the top. We'd never seen a hay stack in our lives. The whole family went, but it didn't feel like working, it was a big adventure. I still go down to Kent now to relive the feeling.'

Families went year after year, even generation after generation to the same farms. According to Stan Little from Canning Town, who was hop-picking in the late 1940s, 'We looked forward every year to the letter coming from the farmer telling us when to go down. I usually went for 12 weeks.' At the time Stan was working for Jeye's Fluid in Plaistow. 'No matter what job I was doing, no matter how good the job, I would always leave so that I could go hopping. I remember once they wanted to promote me to foreman. I told the boss, Mr Bellamy, I couldn't do the job. He couldn't believe it, he asked me if I'd been offered a better post somewhere else. I said, "It's not that, I've just got to go hopping!"'

It was rough country living and most of the hoppers camped in small huts with few amenities provided. Pickers would bring their own bedding and utensils. 'It was just like a pig sty, it was a simple little

Below: hop-picking was the traditional English version of the French 'vendages' grape harvest.

HOLIDAYS ON A SHOESTRING

square hut which had one bed from one side to another made up of last year's vines plus straw,' says Stan Little. 'We always took down this thing called a big tick – a big white sheet sewn together that you filled with straw. It would cover the whole of the bed. We all slept in that one bed.'

Stan's son Dave remembers, 'It was terrible, we had to sleep on these rough old things that were full of straw, and by September it was getting chilly at night. It was all really basic but somehow that added to the charm of it.' Cooking was just as tough. Stan's wife would cater for the family of six on a small Primus stove.

The hopping day started early for Stan, 'I nearly always had a bit of toast over an open fire before the day began about 7.30 and then I'd take a billy can up to the field and start picking. You got paid by the bushel. A tractor would come along and count each basket and empty it. But there was a wonderful atmosphere of friendliness. There were always people laughing as they worked. You were never lonely, you only had to start singing and then someone on the next bin would sing and before you know it, the whole field would be singing and it'd go on all day long. *When we went down hopping, hopping down in Kent. Saw old Mother Riley living in a tent.* There must have been something in those hops!'

Above: Modern, lightweight tents allow campers to hike into remote areas such as this picturesque spot in the Brecon Beacons.

For many, including the Little family, the highlight of the hopping holiday was the evenings around the camp fire. Stan remembers, 'People from the next fire would come and sit with you and you'd be swapping tales and chatting. We'd drink the local scrumpy, it was really strong and before you knew it guitars would come out and you'd start singing. We'd do barbecues, baked apples that we'd nicked from the orchards. The camaraderie was brilliant and it was so beautiful, you know, sitting in the cold night air warming yourself in front of a crackling fire.'

Hop-picking was a passion of many East End families, but the Kent villagers often treated the invading hoppers with suspicion. 'The local people didn't trust us Londoners, there was a lot of tension,' says Lola Smith. 'As far as they were concerned we were all little Artful Dodgers. When we went into the pubs the glasses the hoppers got would have a painted bottom and they'd make you pay a shilling deposit for it. They thought we'd nick the glasses. There would even be notices saying "saloon bar – no hoppers." The local kids would go back to school before we did, so they'd be dressed up in their school uniforms staring at us and shouting, "Oi, look at those horrible cockneys."'

Dave Little loved hopping so much as a teenager that he would dream up schemes to stay on longer in Kent. 'I'd miss the beginning of the school term in September going hopping and that made it worse in a way going back to school at the end of the hop-picking season. I hated it. I'd get this horrible feeling in my stomach of going back to reality and having to start fighting with all the bullies again. One year when I was 13 I was on my way to school with a couple of mates and I suddenly said, "I can't stand this, I want to go back to Kent." So I hitch-hiked up to the Blackwall Tunnel and got down to the farmer's door in Staplehurst. He said, "What are you doing here, you've only just gone back?" I said I couldn't stand school and that I was 16 and wanted a job on the farm. He told me to go and wait in the apple shed and that he'd sort something out. But then he bolted us in and phoned the police.'

His father, Stan, recalls, 'The next thing I knew, I had a call from the police. I had to go down and pick him up. I was hopping mad, but by the time I got down and had cooled off I thought, well, I probably would have done the same.'

Despite the annual truancy, much disapproved of by the school authorities, the skills Dave learnt on his summer holiday job shaped his future career. 'I had always had a natural sort of mechanical brain, mending lawnmowers and stuff, so when I went hopping, the farmer trusted me to do jobs on his old tractor and I suppose he was getting cheap labour out of it. But I learnt how to fix motors and later on I became a mechanic. In fact, I learnt much more from hop-picking than I ever did from school.'

Above: Camping has proved to be the perfect way for young people to follow the rock festival circuit in Britain each summer.

In the 1960s mechanisation rapidly killed off hop-picking holidays as the cost of picking by hand was double that of using a machine. The second agricultural revolution transformed farming all over Britain, reducing the need for manual labour at harvest time. It was the end of an era and by the late 60s the working holiday in the countryside had almost vanished, surviving only with student holiday jobs on fruit picking farms.

Camping, however, was becoming increasingly popular, although its fans were changing. Many of the old enthusiasts had moved on to the safer pleasures of caravanning or were venturing abroad. The camping holiday was also going upmarket. Sites were smartened up and tighter regulations demanded higher standards of accommodation. With the invention of waterproof, man-made fibres and flexible tent poles, tents became a bit more comfortable, sophisticated and expensive. But tents were still cheap enough for young people to buy and from the 70s onwards a new generation of girls and boys who had been brought up as Boy Scouts and Girl Guides began to subvert the old, conservative camping tradition in Britain. As they grew into their teens, they discovered that camping was the perfect way of travelling around on the cheap, following the new rock festival circuit every summer. Spending summer nights in a tent has now become more associated with rock music, sex and drugs than campfires, melted marshmallows and dib, dib, dib. Not at all what Baden-Powell would have imagined.

THE CARAVAN CRAZE

L ike mowing the lawn, digging the allotment and washing the car, caravanning is a quintessentially British pastime. Over the years the British have taken caravanning to their hearts, as can be seen from the long caravan strips strung out along the coast and the great array of mobile homes wintering in front gardens all over the country. One family in five spends its holidays on a caravan site and hundreds of thousands head for the sun every year with a caravan in tow, hogging the slow lane of the M5. The Caravan Club of Great Britain, established in 1907, is the largest caravanning organisation of its kind in the world and has nearly a million members.

The joy of caravanning was the freedom it offered. Christine Fagg has been a devotee of caravan holidays for almost 50 years. 'Caravanning gave you the freedom to take to the road and just get up and go. If you didn't like the site, you could move to another one; if you heard that the weather was bad you could go somewhere where the sun was out; if you liked a place you could stay a few days longer.'

Independence was important, too. No longer were you tied to the landlady's clock, having to get back for mealtimes and sharing a table with people you didn't know and might not like. With a caravan you could please yourself, cook your own food, get up whatever time you wanted to; in short you had freedom to roam. For Lloyd Brown, another caravan crusader, now on the brink of his 90s with over 40 years caravanning behind him, 'It was a wonderful life, you were so free, the air was fresh, you could stop wherever you wanted to.'

Caravans have been around in one form or another since the invention of the wheel. The horse-drawn caravan began to emerge early in the 19th century as a vehicle for travelling showmen and by the end of the century had been adopted by gypsy travellers. Leisure then was something largely restricted to the upper classes and they

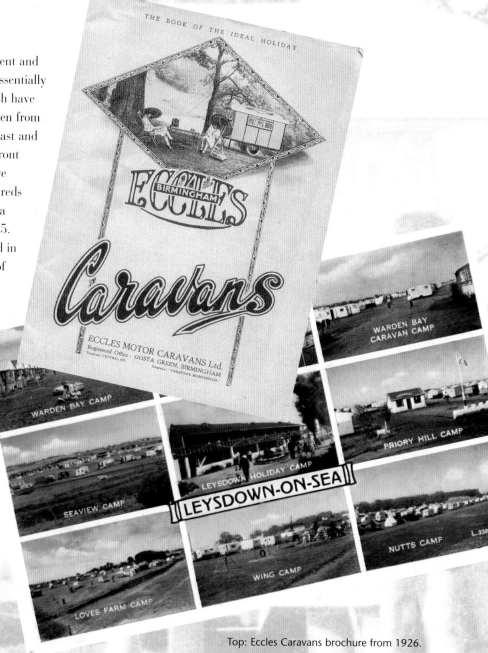

Top: Eccles Caravans brochure from 1926.

Above: A 1961 postcard showing caravans much in evidence at Leysdown-on-Sea in Kent.

took to caravanning like a toff to sherry. A new breed of 'gentlemen gypsies' enjoyed the Romany lifestyle travelling the length and breadth of the country to explore the countryside and stay with their chums. Dr Gordon Stables, an eccentric Victorian author of boys' books, had a horse-drawn caravan built for his personal use. He caught the attention of the nation with the caravan he named *The Wanderer*, a forerunner of the modern leisure caravan. In 1886 he set off in the 2 ton luxury 'land yacht' to tour Britain with a valet on a tricycle in tow. The book of the journey *The Cruise of the Land Yacht Wanderer* did much to bring caravanning to a wider public.

The days of horse power (the four legged variety), however, were fast running out as the internal combustion engine caught on and by the end of World War I motor vehicles had become more powerful and reliable. The next stage was to build a caravan that could be pulled by a car. Many enthusiasts had a go using spare parts left over from the war. In 1919 Capt. St. Barbe Baker of the Royal Flying Corps constructed a caravan made entirely from aeroplane parts and his model is regarded as the first post-World War I trailer caravan. Caravan manufacturing got going after the war drawing on the ample supply of practical ex-servicemen with a wealth of experience of motor vehicles. One of the big names, Eccles, based in Birmingham, started in 1919. Their early designs were quite primitive and they had some difficulty convincing the public that their models, which were little more than sheds on wheels, would provide an enjoyable introduction to a new recreational activity. The original Eccles trailer caravan was not only intended for holidays but also to serve as a mobile doctor's or dentist's surgery in remote areas.

Caravanning grew in the interwar years as the motoring revolution spread through the country. It became part of a romantic notion of getting out onto the road, people talked about being 'motor gypsies' or 'savouring the gypsy joys of caravanning' and early models were like country cottages on wheels with imitation tile roofs, pitched roofs, half timbering, fancy bay windows and leaded light windows. Many of them were designed with little or no thought having been given as to whether they could be safely towed. A few new makes came onto the scene like Cheltenham, Car Cruiser, Winchester and Raven, but most caravans were made to order and caravanning remained predominantly a rich man's pursuit.

Most attention was paid to the inside of the van. Hot and cold water, the wireless, full electrical installations and even baths gave an air of good living and innovation but also added to the weight. As yet there were no sophisticated towbars and with the speed limit for caravans being just 30 miles per hour, the caravan was already developing a reputation for being a slow coach. There were no caravan sites to speak of so it was a case of stopping for the night just about anywhere you fancied, and

Above: A toilet tent containing an Elsan loo was a great convenience but, as many caravanners were to discover, it created its own problems, too.

THE CARAVAN CRAZE

farms were a favourite place to camp.

Caravanning in the 1930s was exclusive, but it wasn't long before the aspiring middle classes started muscling in on this most refined of pastimes. They began to join the ranks of the Caravan Club – you had to be proposed by an existing member so that the right sort of person would join. Caravanning was becoming a more sociable pursuit and annual rallies were introduced in 1932, the first one held at Minehead. At the rallies, caravanners could get together, give each other advice and swap tales of life on the road. Around 90 vans turned up, striking fear into the hearts of local seaside landladies who feared for their businesses. Members would take their evening dress to the rallies and emerge from their vans attired in white tie and tails or long dresses. The Caravan Club adopted the slogan 'Hoot and pass, cheerio!' soothing the irate car owners who got stuck behind a van.

Eccles of Birmingham (telegram address – 'For Caravans, Phone Birmingham') lured more and more people into the joys of the open road during the 1930s, making cheaper and more affordable caravans than ever before. They introduced the National, a 14-foot, four berth caravan which sold for only £130. It was mass-produced, batch built and jig-assembled with a streamlined production process that heralded a new kind of cheap family caravan in marked contrast to the Winchester, the Rolls Royce of caravans, which was individually constructed by craftsmen to high coachbuilding standards.

Above: Having turned left at Calais, Lloyd Brown and his wife ventured as far as the Arctic Circle.

Caravans did their patriotic bit during World War II. On the home front, many were used as air raid shelters in the countryside and as temporary accommodation for evacuees. Caravans were converted into army ambulances, canteens and used as mobile billets for soldiers. Manufacturers turned out functional vans to be of service to the country and the people. The oak panelling, latticed windows and fine tapestries of the upmarket 30s caravan were of little use. When hostilities were over, caravans were needed to house the bombed-out homeless and as temporary homes for workers involved in reconstructing Britain. Shanty towns of caravans became a common sight along main roads and caravans came into their own as mobile homes. In 1946 72% of Eccles caravans were being used as residences, while in 1950 it was estimated that 50% of all caravans were occupied as permanent homes.

The British love affair with caravans really took off during the 1950s. In the austerity years after World War II, rationing was still in force, money was tight and people were having to make do. Holidays abroad were still beyond the reach of most people but caravanning at home was the ideal, low-budget holiday for more adventurous middle class families. For caravanner Christine Fagg, 'It was such a difficult time. If you had a lot of children as we did, caravanning was one of the few holidays that you could possibly think of. Caravanning lent itself so perfectly to not being extravagant. You could save the pennies by buying local produce from farmers and doing things like sticking bits of soap together to make them last longer.'

As the country became more affluent in the 1950s and 60s, the boom in car ownership brought the joys of caravanning within reach of even more people. Within 20 years caravanning established itself as one of the most popular forms of holidaymaking. By the early 1960s there were 75,000 touring caravans, 10,000 motor caravans and another quarter of a million permanently on site as holiday homes in Britain. The new demand for caravans was fed by cheaper vans rolling off the assembly lines. Mass-produced models started to emerge from factories using newly available materials like aluminium. As prices dropped, leisure caravanning became more popular and the Caravan Club doubled its membership during the 60s. Touring was becoming more fashionable and Alperson established itself as a leading player in the market by introducing a simple, hardboard-panelled 11-foot box on wheels named the Sprite. Its creator, Sam Alper, brought it to public attention by embarking on a series of extensive European jaunts which publicised the Sprite's ability to tour long distances. All of this made the Sprite one of the best-known makes of caravan.

There were some wacky caravans, too, like the amphibious caravan which was half boat, half caravan. The Raven Duck created a real buzz in 1950: it was constructed for customers who wanted to combine sailing with caravanning. Its 20-foot body could be removed from the chassis, ready for launching. Another caravan-cum-boat of the same era was the suitably named Otter and later the Gull. The manufacturer, Berkeley, created the Statesman, a revolutionary two-storey caravan with an upstairs bedroom. The British sense of inventiveness was shining through, but the more eccentric designs would not enjoy widespread success.

Caravan sites were now becoming well established, most having developed from simple beginnings in the corners of fields. Over 200 sites were run by the Caravan Club alone and there were thousands of 'certificated locations' dotted around Britain. These were sites of natural beauty, generally on farms, and were restricted to five caravans at any one time. Caravan sites would soon become a permanent feature of the British coastline creating a sprawl for hundreds of miles with particular concentrations in North Wales and Devon. For many, the new sites were an ugly eyesore, blighting the beauty and tranquility of our rural heritage. As social commentator Ray Gosling put it, 'Where once sheep and cows grazed, now farmers milk the caravans.'

Many of the early post-war sites had an extraordinarily ramshackle appearance, with a hotchpotch of ancient caravans hugging the coast. In the late 1950s, Ed Mitchell gave up camping in favour of a cheap, second-hand caravan. 'I bought it off our district nurse. It wasn't so much a caravan as a tin box on wheels, it was made of sheet iron. Well, I saw Jockey Reynolds, the farmer on the campsite where we'd stayed

Above: Bill Haddon built his own luxury caravan in the 1950s.

THE CARAVAN CRAZE

at Overstrand, lovely little place on the Norfolk coast and I said I wanted to put it there. "That'll be six pounds a year, boy," he said, "take it or leave it." So I took it. I'd graduated from camping to caravanning then, but only just. We had to cook outside on a table and on a Primus at first. We didn't have Calor gas cooking. Then I built a little lean-to kitchen by the door. Well, after that tin box we went up to a four berth Pemberton that had a coal fire in it. We thought that was luxury then. There were more caravans coming on the site then but it was still pretty old fashioned.'

Caravanning during the pioneering days was described as 'upmarket tenting.'

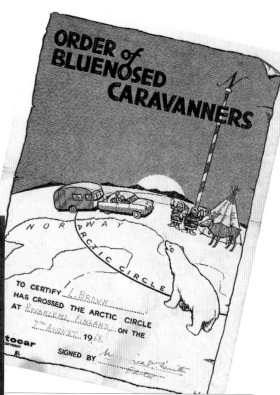

Get away from the chimneys.

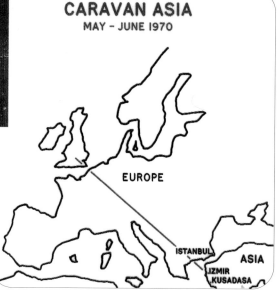

CARAVAN ASIA
MAY – JUNE 1970

As with camping you had to take the rough with the smooth and laugh off the hiccups. One of the biggest difficulties was the lack of modern toilet facilities in caravans and on campsites. Many a time an intrepid caravanner has relieved himself in the corner of a field. Early caravans often had the most basic of sanitary equipment and what was the unmentionable was also the invisible. Toilet tents (with bucket) were often set up hidden away in bushes. Ann Hasler recalls making do in the 1950s. 'My parents bought an Eccles caravan to tow behind our Morris car. On one holiday we went to Pembrokeshire and pitched the caravan on a cliff edge near Tenby where we had a magnificent view. The Elsan tent was put up, not a proper one, just a white conventional canvas tent with huge wooden pegs and thick guy ropes. It looked really secure. The Elsan, a glorified bucket with a sort of seat and lid on it, was ceremoniously placed in the centre of the tent, with a spade positioned close by for later use, and a can of Jeyes fluid. A few days passed by until the weather took a turn for the worse. The shipping forecast said that we were to expect Force 10 gales in the next 24 hours – and we got one. It blew a gale and in the middle of the night my father had to move the caravan to a more sheltered spot, but by the morning the gale had blown itself out. Naturally, when we got up we needed to visit the Elsan tent but when we opened the curtains there was no sign of it. We soon found out that the tent had been torn from its pegs and was now dangling perilously

Top left: 1929 Car Cruiser caravan brochure.

Top: Lloyd Brown's certificate celebrating his intrepid journey.

Above: A memento of an epic caravan expedition to another continent.

down the cliff, just held by some brambles. The Elsan had been blown down the field, conveniently emptying itself on the way, but the spade and can of fluid had not moved!'

Margaret Butcher from Norfolk also had problems with her Elsan loo. 'We were in Scotland towing our somewhat primitive caravan uphill on the narrow road towards a small hotel. Heading towards us was a large coach destined to pick up the group of tourists waiting by the roadside. There was insufficient room to pass and my husband stopped the car with less than his normal smooth style. The resulting jerk caused our Elsan loo – which in the absence of the en-suite shower rooms of today's caravans was fastened onto the towbar – to fall onto the road, whereupon it rolled back down the hill, losing its lid and spreading its noisome contents over the tarmac in the process!

'I happened to be wearing an extremely smart, new cream trouser suit that day, not at all the type of garment for loo-chasing, but as my husband could hardly continue to block the road, I felt obliged to leap after the thing, scooping up as much of the mess as possible with a convenient stick. The speed with which I ran back to the car on completing the task would have impressed any Olympic talent scout!'

Another hazard was torrential rain which could quickly flood primitive caravan sites, many of which had little or no drainage. In hours they could became quagmires, making it impossible for the touring caravan to move. And although caravans provided a lot more protection from the elements than a tent, inexperienced caravanners were extremely vulnerable to heavy downpours. Shirley Smith's first experience was so sodden that it nearly put her off for life. With her husband, 'Mr Fix-It' and children she set off for a farmsite at Bolton-le-Sands. 'Dusk fell and we discovered how cosy it was sitting in our van listening to the gentle patter of the rain on the roof. The children couldn't wait to try out their bunk beds and soon settled down into their sleeping bags. I checked them later and discovered they were getting wet; rain was coming in through the window. So Mr Fix-It rigged up a remarkable contraption with plastic sheeting. The rain went on and it wasn't long before I stretched my legs and discovered my own sleeping bag was wet. I woke Mr Fix-It to tell him of this event only to be told, "Well, bend your knees!" At 2 a.m. I woke him again and demanded to be taken home. He wasn't having that, but he did rouse himself enough to fit another plastic sheet which caught the rain and fed it back out at the bottom of the window.

'Dawn broke, we all scampered off to have showers and the night's trauma really didn't seem so bad. My first job was to dismantle the plastic sheeting but too late came the warning from Mr Fix-It. I unhooked the wrong end first and the reservoir of water cascaded all over me and the bed. Meanwhile, my daughter needed to go to the toilet. It was so ancient, it should have been in a museum. I leant over her to flush the loo and a fountain of water shot out of the cistern completely over my daughter's head and yes, soaked me again. As I'd used up all my spare clothing I had to travel back feeling very damp.' Despite this experience, more than 30 years on, the Smiths are still caravanning and, five caravans later, now have a luxury two berth with all mod cons and no leaks of any kind.

Above: Sallie Haddon serves tea in her home-from-home.

THE CARAVAN CRAZE

Carry On Camping style mishaps, the more serious struggle against the elements and coping with a lack of basic facilities on many sites all helped to forge a strong spirit of camaraderie, fondly remembered by many early caravanners. 'There was a wonderful atmosphere amongst the caravanners in those days,' says Ed Mitchell. 'If you had a problem, if something went wrong, which it did all the time, it was part of the fun to help each other out. We did everything together. Like with cricket, I'd go round all the caravans knocking on the doors saying, "Everybody out for cricket!" and everyone would join in. I had a very loud voice and they called me the Sergeant Major. Then I'd say, "Right let's all play volleyball," or all of a sudden, "Everybody in the sea." God we used to have a lovely time there at Overstrand.'

While the majority still took their holiday renting a caravan on a fixed site, by the 1960s more and more were aspiring to buy their own van and go touring. This growing demand further boosted the British caravan industry. Sprite became the global name in caravans and through buy-outs came to dominate the budget end of the market at home and abroad. Their models, from the Alpine to the Major, the Colt and the Musketeer, became synonymous with touring caravans. The Alpine, a 12-foot tourer, became the bestselling caravan of all time. Luxury caravan makers did well too; Carlight, Stirling, Welton and other names such as Cheltenham were the tourers people dreamed of. And Britain acquired a caravan manufacturing capital – Hull – which had the largest concentration of makers including Swift, Ace, Mardon and Silverline.   Creature comforts were extended as well, making the caravan even more of a mobile home from home. The super luxury tourers boasted new facilities like hot and cold water, showers, fridges, ovens, double-glazing, heating, an awning and lavatories.

The intrepid British spirit was busy, too, using DIY skills to construct homemade caravans. Most of those who embarked on this course were couples devoted to caravanning, but who could not afford to buy one. In the 1950s Graham and Christine Fagg from Hertfordshire converted an ex-army ambulance into their first caravan. Around the same time Bill and Sallie Haddon of Birmingham had a dream of building their own luxury caravan. He worked as a lorry driver and she as a shop assistant. Undeterred by lack of funds they resolved that their DIY caravan would 'have the best of everything.' Starting with a chassis, they put on a framework, woodwork, aluminium on the outside and teak formica on the inside. They installed a fridge, toilet, a big wardrobe with a full-length mirror and the ultimate luxury of a cocktail cabinet. Embroidered vinyl decorated the walls and the windows had 'swish little curtains.' They became the envy of the caravan site they frequented in the Forest of Dean, but unfortunately

Below: A 1928 Eccles on site with a 1936 Triumph Southern Cross parked alongside.

Above: Christine Fagg with the caravan she towed behind her Volkswagen Beetle.

the caravan was so laden with luxury goods, it could barely be towed. It acquired the nickname 'The Elephant.'

The Lentons of Wakefield were just as enterprising. They ran a family haulage business and in the 60s as money was short, they decided to convert one of their lorries into a makeshift caravan by throwing a tarpaulin over the iron bars on top. They furnished it with a fitted carpet, sofas, a bed-settee for the parents and bunk beds for the children. They added a chest of drawers and a calor gas stove, named it 'The Wagon' and off they went around Britain. According to Betty Lenton, 'We chose "The Wagon" because everything could go in. When we were setting off the children would ask if they could take their bikes and in they went with all the dollies, the prams and anything else which wouldn't have fitted into a caravan. We rarely went on official caravan sites because people would stare and say, "Oh my God, what's this coming in?" They were probably thinking, "Hello, who are these undesirables?" We didn't care, though, we just went elsewhere. We never knew where we were heading for, we were just free spirits. Ronnie, my husband, was the driver, I was the navigator and the children would ride in the back and wave to cars on the road. It was a wonderful, unique holiday and the main thing was that we were together as a family.'

The Lentons would stop for the night on farmland, 'If you asked the farmer nicely, it was rare that you'd be refused.' Once, however, it went badly wrong. 'We went up in "The Wagon" to Scotland and came across a beautiful loch. It was so peaceful and the birds were singing so we thought, "Let's spend the night here." We went to bed and all at once, the next morning, there was this banging on the side of "The Wagon"

THE CARAVAN CRAZE

and when Ronnie pulled the canvas back to look out there were these four men and they all had shotguns pointing at us. Well, I was absolutely terrified, I thought they were going to shoot us. One of the farmers said, "What d'you think you're doing, you're on my land? We don't like your sort around." So in my best posh voice I said, "What do you mean, 'our sort.' We have a perfectly decent car at home, we're just on holiday in 'The Wagon,' we're not doing any harm." But he was quite scary and even though he'd mistaken us for travelling people we weren't going to hang around.' Not wanting to argue with shotguns they moved on pretty sharpish.

Moving into the 70s, the caravanning press confirmed that 'the touring caravan explosion shows no sign of abating.' With the growth in touring, many caravanners became more adventurous and left home territory to head overseas. Lloyd Brown from Hertfordshire would get off the ferry at Calais and ask his wife, 'Shall we turn left or right this time?' and then strike out at random through France or off towards the North. Lloyd must take one of the prizes for long distance touring, in the 1960s and 70 he ventured deep into the Communist Bloc as far as the Russian border, up through Scandinavia 400 miles into the Arctic Circle, down to Morocco and 8000 miles coast to coast in the States. His most dramatic experience, though, was in Spain in the 60s.

'We were returning from a trip to Morocco when we decided to spend a few days at Las Palmeras, a caravan site situated between Alicante and Benidorm. It was a black, rainy night when we arrived at about 10 p.m. We drove through bushes and trees in torrential rain towards the lights of the campsite ahead where we had to cross the Alicante-Benidorm Lemon Express railway line. Suddenly there was a bang and the caravan was stuck in the centre of the rails. For some 20 minutes I tried to reverse, I tried rocking the caravan back and forth, the clutch smelt awful and panic was rising for fear of the train coming. We were desperate. Suddenly people turned up from the caravan site and, with a struggle, we managed to unhitch the caravan and turn it off the railway line. Within five minutes of moving it off, sweat still pouring, the train belted along between the caravan and the car.

Above: Preparing a meal in the open air at the Caravan Club's site near Marlow in Buckinghamshire.

'With terrific rain and so much thunder and lightning the whole of Alicante Electrics broke down leaving the town in complete darkness, but we were lucky, we had gas lighting in the van and could still see around. It turned out that the owner of the campsite had rung Alicante station and stopped the Lemon Express in its path. We rehitched the van and I went to thank the people who had saved us from disaster. I was quite ill with stomach pains for a week afterwards – I believed it was from the shock but my wife claimed it was the sangria I drank after the event! It was so frightening, but afterwards I was reminded of all those silent films where Mary Pickford or Charlie Chaplin were tied to the railway line.'

Sallie Haddon with her husband, Bill, spent a summer holiday in the 70s touring the Alps in their beloved homemade van 'The Elephant.' Going up over an alpine pass in Switzerland, it started to snow. They were having trouble towing 'The Elephant' up the mountain and the truck in front was going so slowly it looked as though it would roll backwards at any moment and crush them. 'Feeling somewhat anxious, I said to Bill, "Let's pull over, I could really do with a cup of tea."' High up on the mountain they pulled into a precariously placed layby and Sallie put the kettle on for a soothing cuppa. Unexpectedly, there came a knock on the door. The police had come to tell them that they had shut down the pass because of the weather. 'But I was so desperate for the tea, I said, "Can we stay until we've finished our cup?"' Time passed, the snow got heavier, the first cup was so good it was followed by a second and before they knew it the police had returned with the news that the pass had been closed. The tea-drinking caravanners were then firmly escorted off the mountain.

Touring could be quite a macho activity, the men hitched the caravans and drove and the women assumed the traditional role of navigator and companion. But women were involved in solo caravanning early on and it wasn't long before they wanted to take the driver's seat. In the Caravan Club in the 1910s, women accounted for nearly a third of the members. Advice was given by 'experienced lady caravanners' such as, 'If you are following a route which includes many towns and have any intention of attending evening entertainments, then an evening dress of non-spoilable, non-crushable description is necessary. Let your skirts be short . . . clear of the ground all round and one or two of just above ankle length for wet or muddy days!'

In the 1960s, Christine Fagg found that caravanning brought new excitement into her life. 'I had to have some other positive interest in my life, other than playing

Above: By the 1970s, some caravans had grown too big for touring and were kept permanently on site as holiday homes.

THE CARAVAN CRAZE

bridge, going to coffee mornings and walking the dog. I wanted to have something I could hang on to. I learnt to tow by watching my husband do everything and then having him sit beside me while I did it. And watching him hitch and unhitch and then doing it myself.' She developed an independent streak. As a young mother of four in the 50s, her paediatrician husband had developed a passion for sailing and took the family away on compulsory seafaring holidays. 'I spent the whole time feeling sick, bored or terrified. And then caravanning came along to my rescue.' With a caravan Christine found a new interest and was able to join her husband on the coast. She maintains that 'caravanning saved my marriage.'

Her first weekend away alone in the early 60s was spent a mere 12 miles from home in Dunstable Downs. 'I felt reborn, a new woman – like I'd been to the North Pole and back.' Christine's new-found freedom coincided with the birth of women's liberation and caused a lot of comment. 'I remember on one of the first trips, I went over a roundabout in Shropshire and a woman started gesticulating at me. I wound down the car window and she shouted, "I wouldn't be in your shoes for all the tea in China." But I absolutely loved it.'

Christine would become a leading light in the caravanning world, carving an unexpected career for herself editing the women's page of Caravan Magazine. 'I was away in the Peak District and one of my friends had left me a pile of old caravanning magazines and I read these articles and I thought I'd never read such boring articles in my life. They were all about about how to improve your undergear or repaint your bodywork. Why on Earth hadn't someone written about how to cope in a caravan with children? On the spur of the moment I contacted the editor of one of the magazines who wrote back and said that such an article might be of interest to ladies like myself who

Below: A cutting from Christine Fagg's Womanwise column and a shot of Christine hard at work in the 'Lady-Go-Lightly.'

Just how versatile is a van?

Friends of mine put their caravan to good use even on the cold night of November 5. As darkness falls, they'll hitch up their caravan to the car and tow it to a farmer's field where fellow Round Tablers and their wives will be preparing a firework bonanza for their children. Here my friends will set up the caravan and heat up vast quantities of soup and fry hot dogs. What bliss it will [be] to creep out of the biting wind into the c[osy] atmosphere inside, even if the aroma [of] onions hangs heavily on the air and cling[s] to clothes and hair long afterwards.

A caravan is so versatile. This same outfi[t] is also taken to our annual donkey derby, where it acts as an office for collecting the money raised for charity. It's also been used as a fortune teller's tent, a bar, and for rendering first-aid at various functions. Another time it housed an exhibition of dolls at a fete and once it even took a prize in a carnival procession, decorated and camouflaged as a porcupine. A caravan lends itself to so many uses in connection with money-raising efforts for charity.

This summer, we took our caravan to attend a wedding about 60 miles away from home. We could have managed the journey in a day, but how much more pleasant it was to stay on for the night, entertain fellow guests and renew old acquaintances during the evening and following day.

And if you're lucky enough to be able to park your caravan in your own garden, isn't it heavenly to dump your summer visitors to sleep in it, especially if you provide breakfast for them to cook for themselves?

Do you put *your* caravan to uses other than holidays? If so, I'd like to h[ear from] them and perhaps we c[an] pooling id[eas]

... tones in the cur ...nat a difference they give to the look and comfort of the place!—See below.

The most popular caravan cushion is the big, square shape into which you pop your pillow and then zip up quickly to disguise it and use by day. But why not make some specially shaped cushions with appropriately decorated covers as shown below, perhaps as a Christmas present for your husband, or a caravanning friend or relative? Details of how to make these cushions can be obtained from me, Christine Fagg, at CARAVAN, Link House Publications Ltd, Dingwall Avenue, Croydon CR9 2TA.

WOMANWISE

Edited by CHRISTINE FAGG

travelled unaccompanied.' She became known as the 'Lady with the Van.'

After years of putting up with caravans that had 'awkward storage and revolting interiors,' Christine took matters in hand and decided to design her own caravan – the result was the aptly named Lady-go-Lightly which was exhibited at Earl's Court in 1980. Christine made it as light as possible so that hitching was easy. 'I wanted the caravan to be bright, vibrant and well-ordered – even the bottle opener had its own special place, and the plate drainer was hidden away in a cupboard.' Christine designed a set of tables that would hook onto each other so that she could even host a dinner party for seven in her van. In her magazine column she suggested ways in which you could get around the problems of catering in a caravan. Recipes were suggested that could be cooked away from home like 'boeuf stroganoff – caravan style'. For Christine, 'Every new advance that the food manufacturers came out with, packets of this, tins of that, I'd leap upon it with glee.'

Caravans have always had their detractors. In the 1980s there was an Anti-Caravan Club formed by a barrister after he became fed up with being caught once too often behind a slow-moving van. An advert was placed in the small ads of *Private Eye* and membership reached over a thousand. The Club was supposed to mount vigilante patrols to mark down caravanners' crimes against motoring. Such criticisms have done little to dampen the popular enthusiasm for caravanning and in recent years it has enjoyed another boom after hitting a stagnant period in the 80s. Sales are picking up again – in 1998 24,000 touring caravans and 20,000 static caravans were sold, some costing over £30,000 with interiors rivalling owners' real homes. Fitted kitchens, air-conditioning, double glazing and central heating are now standard. Gone are the days of simply hitching up. Now you pull into a park and plug into satellite television, water and electricity. Caravanning is also losing its naff image and becoming cool, popular amongst families who like the great outdoors and relish the ability to get off the beaten track. Many who sneered at the van when they were forced into it as a teenager back in the 60s are now proud caravanners themselves.

Caravanning has always meant so much more than a holiday to the British, it is more a way of life. The importance of caravanning can be seen in one example alone. Lloyd Brown's wife, Lyn, was diagnosed with multiple sclerosis in 1960. Lloyd was called into the doctor's surgery and told to 'make the best of the next five years.' Shocked, Lloyd and Lyn took the doctor's advice, sold their newsagent's business, bought a caravan and went off touring around the world. The caravan, with its bed in the back, was perfect, whenever his wife was tired, Lloyd pulled over to the side of the road and let her rest. They spent the next few years on the road travelling across nearly every continent in the world. When they eventually returned to the specialists they were told that they had done the right thing. With the adjustments they had made to their diet and the fresh air caravanning, 'it was the perfect way of life.' They were still caravanning 40 years later. What did caravanning mean to the Browns? 'Salvation. It meant everything to us. It saved us from a dreadful time. We've enjoyed so many wonderful holidays together, just living for the moment, and the fun has just gone on and on.'

Above: Lloyd and Lyn Brown were among the most adventurous of touring caravan enthusiasts.

THE LURE OF THE MEDITERRANEAN

I n 1956 the cult film *And God Created Woman* turned Brigitte Bardot into a world famous star and sexual icon. It also popularised sun worship and put St Tropez on the map with its voluptuous, bronzed women and nude sunbathing. It was here on the French Riviera that young women had shocked the world ten years earlier by daringly revealing the latest in swimwear – the bikini. It was the skimpiest two-piece swimsuit ever designed and was first sold – and worn – in Cannes. In the years following World War II, the Cote d'Azur was regarded as a land of beautiful people and glamorous film stars, living the good life in a paradise of sun, sea and sand. This was where Hollywood stars like Humphrey Bogart and Rita Hayworth bought their luxurious second homes, where Hollywood princess Grace Kelly met her fairytale prince and where the glitterati sipped cocktails on their quayside yachts. It was a magnet to millions of tourists and a younger generation of Britons dreamt of a holiday where they could see and be seen on the Mediterranean. The great allure of the Riviera was its elegance and style, together with a frisson of erotic and exotic pleasure far more dangerous and exciting than anything on offer at home.

Kathy Vyse, a typist from South Wales, planned a trip to Nice in 1957 with her friends. 'We used to love going to the cinema every Saturday. I was a big fan of the movies, we really idolised the stars. When I turned 18 I decided that I wanted to go to the Riviera to experience the glamour for myself. I thought that the *Promenade des Anglais* would be paved with film stars! It took me six months to save up for a week in Nice. We went from Heathrow, stopping off at Orly for refuelling. When we arrived at Nice airport the first person I saw was Lex Barker who played Tarzan. It made my

Above left: In the 1950s, beachwear was becoming recognisably modern as demonstrated by these ads for swimsuits and suntan lotion.

Above: Travelling to the South of France was a major undertaking up to the 1960s, but determined British holidaymakers persevered.

82

holiday before it had even started!'

The warm, balmy, lemon-scented climate enjoyed by the French Riviera had long attracted holiday-makers not only from Britain, but from and all over the world. It had first proved popular – along with the Italian Riviera – as a stopping off point on the Grand Tour, the cultural journey around continental Europe that was one of the rites of passage of young English gentlemen in the 17th and 18th centuries. The transformation into a tourist hot spot really started in the 1850s with the arrival of the railway. Then it replaced Italy as the home-from-home for well-heeled Brits. Aged wealthy visitors in search of health cures for consumption were followed by social climbers and pleasure seekers. By late Victorian times the area had become highly fashionable among the English aristocracy and royalty, who migrated south in late September, staying until April when they left their continental villas to return home for the society 'season.'

Until the 1930s the Riviera was essentially a winter resort considered by the pale-faced migrants to be oppressively hot in the summer months. In July and August resorts like Nice and Cannes were largely deserted. It was only during the inter-war years that this stretch of coastline became popular in the summer when sunbathing and seabathing came into vogue. The old conventional wisdom had been that the very hot sun and the foreign waters were unsuitable and potentially damaging to the British tourist. Though many new hotels were built and the old ones now stayed open throughout the summer season, up to the 1950s the Riviera remained an expensive and exclusive aristocratic playground. Only well-to-do Britons could afford to holiday there. And because they served a small, monied class, there were very few resorts on the French Mediterranean coast.

In the post-war years, however, the new, glamorous, starry image of the South of France, combined with its illustrious aristocratic and cultural heritage, exercised a strong pull on many Brits of modest means. Tantalised by cinema films, travelogues featuring globetrotters jetting in and gossip columns all extolling the Riviera as the epicentre of chic, they wanted to see it and experience it for themselves. It grew into one of the most popular destinations for Britons holidaying

Below: Lex Barker, who played Tarzan, snapped by Kathy Vise at Nice Airport in 1957.

Bottom: It took Kathy six months to save up for a week's holiday in Nice.

THE LURE OF THE MEDITERRANEAN

Left: The casino at Monte Carlo was regularly visited by English gentlemen on their 'Grand Tour.'

abroad. World War II had broadened the nation's horizons, taking millions of men abroad in the armed services and removing women from a narrow homelife to do war work. There was a new confidence to break with tradition and aspire to a different kind of holiday. Britons started contemplating holidays abroad. Dorothy Isles was a secretary living with her husband, a textiles foreman, in the mill town of Kirkham in Lancashire when, in August 1957, she decided to break with the local custom of Wakes Weeks holidays. 'It was like going to the moon,' says Dorothy. 'Nobody had ever been to France for a holiday where we lived. They all went to Blackpool. They were very worried for us and my parents were horrified. They'd never heard of anyone going abroad except in a war. They made us so worried that we made a will the day before we left.'

To aspirational singles, couples and families it seemed a great adventure to travel to the South of France, a land so different from the austerity of Britain, to taste some of its pleasures, to enjoy guaranteed sunshine in the Mediterranean and to rub shoulders with the rich and famous. At the very least they hoped to come back with a suntan, an impressive list of sights seen and a fund of stories to entertain family and friends. There was sometimes also a more serious purpose, deeply felt after World War II – to learn about different nations and cultures and to reach out the hand of friendship to help ensure that the world would never again have to endure such a devastating conflict. Idealists like Lucy Mason from Hampshire were helped by the widespread popularity of the British in France immediately after the war. 'We'd liberated them, we'd been a very important ally to them and they loved the British just after the war. They couldn't do enough for you. We always had a Union Jack on our packs as our family walked or cycled around. And they'd make the V for Victory sign like Churchill did whenever they saw it. They were only too pleased to help direct you or give you what you wanted.' According to Lucy's husband, Perry, 'I remember we were out on our cycles one day and we came to a crossroads with a gendarme directing the traffic. We were sort of in convoy – well, of course, we had the Union Jacks on, which was the common thing with people going abroad in those days and as soon as the gendarme saw us, oh, he blew his whistle and stopped all the traffic each side. "Monsieur, come along, come along, vive Churchill," and a salute, you know, we couldn't go wrong.'

Whatever the motive, for the majority of Britons getting to the South of France in the 1950s was still extremely difficult. Of the half million or so who went there every year, very few went on the scheduled flights which were then forbiddingly expensive and largely restricted to businessmen. Coach trips to the Mediterranean offered by tour operators like Thomas Cook were more popular but they, too, were pricey and the accommodation was often at hotels which were really beyond the pocket of most holidaymakers. The most attractive and economical option for many was to go under their own steam. This being the age of the motorcar, driving down through France became a viable proposition for middle-class families. The more affluent and aspirational working classes were also buying second-hand cars and becoming more mobile than ever before.

Determined motorists unable to afford a new car undertook the journey in ageing, patched up, second-hand vehicles. Most drove to the coastal ports and took a car ferry to France. There was also a minority of even

Right: The rapid spread of car ownership throughout the 1950s and 60s inspired adventurous motorists to travel beyond France, with Italy becoming a popular destination.

more ambitious travellers who decided to go by train, by bicycle or on foot, or a combination of all these means. Others made for the smaller airports on the south coast like Lydd in Kent looking for a cheap, short-distance flight across the Channel.

THE LURE OF THE MEDITERRANEAN

In the immediate post-war years there were many small independent British airlines, most of them 'seat-of-the-pants' affairs founded by ex-RAF pilots with a couple of surplus DC-3 aircraft bought from the Air Ministry. Services often ran on an *ad hoc* basis and some travellers just turned up without any prior booking, hoping for the best, then did a deal with the pilot. There was none of the paperwork, the safeguards

Left and bottom left: The Mason Family had a hair-raising experience crossing the Channel in an ex-RAF transport plane, but they made it!

and the complex organisation that came to characterise airports and holidays abroad from the 1960s onwards. Lucy Mason first flew across the Channel in 1949 on a family holiday travelling by foot and by train in France. 'It was just a gamble really. We'd heard that former RAF pilots were running planes

Below: The Isles' family car suffered greatly in the heat on continental trips.

to Le Touquet in France from Lydd airport, so we went down there in the car. It wasn't so much an airport as an old shed. There was no customs, nothing, and we spoke to a pilot and he said he'd take us over with all the newspapers and mail he'd be carrying. So we said yes, we saw an old chappie leaning over a garden gate and we

Right: For the Field family the entire journey, including the boys' novel in-car toilet facilities, was one big adventure.

asked him to look after our car if we left it
with him. We paid ten shillings (50 pence)
each then we got on board, and my heart was in my boots
because I'd never flown before! That plane was so old, the
seating was very rough inside, it was really and truly held
together with hope and goodwill, but we made it.'

Those who wanted to take their cars by the fastest possible
route across the Channel flew the 'air ferry.' Britain pioneered
air ferry services in 1948 with planes carrying two vehicles to
France on each trip. By the late 1950s, services were operating

THE LURE OF THE MEDITERRANEAN

from Southend, Lydd and Bournemouth airports. The cost of an all-in return to Le Touquet was £25 and the journey time was around 50 minutes. In 1958 over 125,000 cars were ferried out of Britain and back by 25 planes. Such was the demand for flying your car to France, bookings had to be made months in advance. It seemed at the time that this was the way in which mass tourism in Europe might develop. A Movietone *Look at Life* newsreel of 1960 titled *The Car Has Wings* trumpeted that air ferries were an exciting new trend that would help shape air travel in the future. The service, however, was never quite as streamlined and glamorous as it claimed to be.

Margaret Maudsley travelled to France on an air ferry in 1959 – within a few years tourist air ferries would go into decline, soon to be consigned to history. 'It was a huge old army transport plane, still painted khaki with army camouflage, all patched up. Well, I didn't think it would ever take off. They put our Dormobile in, it was one of about six cars, chained them up, then we got in. It was all very rough. You sat on the floor on these old army seats with your knees up to your chin. When we took off it shook and rattled something terrible, it didn't go very high. You were just skimming the water. I never thought we'd make it. The air ferry was something I never wanted to travel on again and we never did, apart from coming back which was equally terrifying.'

On arrival in France the first challenge facing travellers was the language. Basic French had long been part of the grammar school curriculum as a second language

Above: Hitch-hiking to the Riviera was one cheap way of sun seeking in the 1950s.

Above: Irene Mayo and Gillian Webb hitched to the South of France spending only £5. Their exploits were featured in the magazine 'Picture Post' in 1954.

and some of the new tourists prided themselves on their ability to converse with 'the natives.' 'It was very important to me to speak in French,' says Pamela Woodland, a former primary school teacher from Lincolnshire. 'I liked it, they liked it and they treated you with more respect as a result. I'd learnt the language when I was young and it came back to me, "oui, merci madame." My motto was, when in Rome do as the Romans do.' But conversational French was, for most British holidaymakers of this generation, long forgotten or non existent. Most remember arriving with just a handful of phrases to help them get by.

Nevertheless this handicap didn't dampen the ardour of internationalists like Lucy Mason, a housewife and mother. 'I could only speak a couple of words but I still felt I could get to know them and make friends. You can communicate a lot with sign language and laughter. We actually felt that by doing this, in some small way we were starting to build a new world where politicians of different nations couldn't declare war on each other any more because the families had met and knew each other.'

Those making the 700 mile journey south by car for the first time faced the challenge of driving on the right hand side and navigating in a foreign country. Fear of disaster helped promote a spirit of camaraderie among the British motorists. 'If you saw another car with a GB sticker, you would always toot them. You were all in it together, you almost wanted to pull over, get out and kiss them,' says Leonard Smith, a former property director from South London who toured the Riviera in 1957. 'And if

Left: Margaret Maudsley thought she was the height of fashion in her white swimsuit in 1958, until she saw the bikini-clad sunbathers in Monte Carlo.

Below: When it was first introduced, even some fashion models refused to wear the new bikini.

Opposite: Bikinis on display outside the Carlton Hotel in Cannes, 1958.

you were feeling a bit lost you'd just follow any car with a GB sticker and hope it was going your way.'

Most who embarked on these touring holidays had very little cash to spare, a situation exacerbated by the tight currency controls which imposed a £30 limit on the amount holidaymakers could take out of Britain. Many could not afford to stay in hotels so they made their own arrangements, sleeping in a tent or in the back of their car. 'I used to sleep on the front seat with a steering wheel up my bottom until I told my husband Leonard that it was his turn to sleep there, then he promptly took it off. I remember every morning he would get up and shave using the wing mirror,' says Pat Smith. There was much scope for mishaps and misunderstandings. Pat recalls the time Leonard innocently parked for the night in a deserted town square. 'We were woken up by this banging on the window and someone shouting, *"Marché! Marché!"* When we looked around we saw we were bang in the middle of a market square and everyone was setting up their stalls. I had no choice but to leap out of the car in my babydoll nightdress, run away and hide.'

One of the main problems facing those who travelled in the height of the summer was the intense heat. It could have a devastating effect on second-hand cars, some of them more than 25 years old. 'It was an old Austin Seven and I think we got about a hundred miles then the radiator overheated badly and the engine went. There was smoke everywhere,' recalls Ronald Briggs from Worcester, who attempted to reach the Riviera in 1950. 'I took it to a garage and they said it was beyond hope. I left it there and had to hitch home.'

Richard Isles, too, faced severe difficulties. 'The heat was unbelievable. It was an

old car and the tyres were old, too. They had inner tubes which were patched up and it got so hot they melted and came off one after the other, so we kept getting flat tyres and we kept having to stop while I pumped them up with the foot pump. Then it got even hotter and the tar on the road was melting and cars were actually getting stuck in the tar. To get round that we travelled early in the mornings when it was cooler. Of course, there was no ventilation and we could only go about 30 m.p.h. so it took several days to get across France. My wife was getting so very fed up, she just wanted to go home. I had to persuade her that we should keep on going.'

When George Field, a self-employed builder, set off from Paignton to the Riviera in 1948, he knew it was an epic journey that needed elaborate planning for it to be a success. He had two young children whom he feared would be constantly demanding toilet stops, thus adding to the time and stress involved. His solution was a very simple yet novel invention. 'We only had an old car, it was an Austin 10 I'd managed to pick up, and I thought, "I'm not going to keep stopping for these children to have a wee." So before we left I drilled a hole in the floor behind the front seats and put a funnel in it. And I said to Christopher and Damon, "When you want to go, just go in the funnel." It worked very well, it really cut down any stops, that funnel must have saved us hours. And as we were driving across France I could hear Damon saying to Christopher, "Don't do it yet until I look out of the back window!" and they'd be watching the wee spraying behind the car as we went along. My wife was a bit worried

about it but anyone who saw the dribbling underneath the car probably thought our radiator had burst.'

George had no qualms about using the French roads as a urinal because, like most of the pioneers who travelled across the Channel in the post-war years, he was shocked by the insanitary condition of continental toilets. 'In France the public toilets were terrible, nothing like what we had at home. You only used them when you had to.'

Pat Smith remembers, 'They were horrific, you walked into a cubicle and there was a hole in the ground, the vilest smelling hole you can imagine and each side there was a porcelain foot print and you placed your feet in them. Then there were two metal bars on either side and you lowered yourself over the hole and just hoped that nothing came up and bit you.'

Odette Lesley recalls, 'We were used to toilets that were private, but when you went through the towns you'd see these toilets and they only had a sort of stable door, so you could see people naked to the world peeing in the loos. And it was a common sight to see them relieving themselves up against walls or in fields. Toilet stops were a source of great anxiety. And you often had to pay to go in, too, and there was one famous occasion where a lady was trapped in the loo because the enormous woman standing guard over it wouldn't let her out because she couldn't pay the two francs you needed to spend rather a big penny. We heard her frantically calling – her husband must have wandered off somewhere and she didn't have any money. So the British

Opposite left: Monte Carlo had long been the preserve of the rich and famous, but from the 1950s onwards it became another stop on the tourist trail.

Above middle: When Pamela Woodland's beachwear left her feeling overdressed, she had no qualms about immediately buying a bikini.

Above: Kathy Vyse on the beach at Calvi in Corsica.

Left: Margaret Rowe, Miss England 1955, models beside a bikini vending machine.

Above: Thomas Cook advertising literature from the 1950s.

people there had a little whip round and got her out.'

Not all of this was prejudice on the part of the Brits. Sanitation and sewage, especially in rural parts of France, were inadequate or nonexistent and generally below the standards established in Britain by the middle of the 20th century. St-Rémy-de-Provence, a beautiful destination in the South of France, had its first sewage system installed in 1956. Even in Paris, the public toilets were considered by many to be shameful and insanitary. During the 1950s there were over 500 *vespasiennes*, places where males were allowed to urinate openly in the streets, protected only by a thin fence. Throughout France public toilets were often extremely primitive and those worst served were women, for whom there were very few decent facilities.

What to eat and where to eat also posed problems for the early British tourists who were often nervous about foreign food. Cashstrapped from the beginning, most of those who went by car took enough supplies to get them down to the South of France. Amongst some there was a siege mentality. Dorothy Isles remembers, 'We'd gone prepared and I'd even boiled a chicken but that went off in the heat and was inedible. We took lots of tinned foods and most of all we ate corned beef. It was always in the back of your mind that the British soldiers had eaten bully beef in France in the World War I and survived, so we could survive on it, too. And that's what we lived on right until we got down to the Riviera.'

Even for those who wanted to experiment by eating out, going into cafés and restaurants could be a daunting prospect. Continental foods were practically unknown in Britain in the 1950s and ordering and eating them was a leap in the dark. 'It took us about a week to work up the courage to eat out,' recalls Pat Smith. 'I asked for a tomato salad and it was the first time I'd ever eaten olive oil. In England you could only buy it in chemists, it was totally medicinal. I loved it.'

Margaret Maudsley ventured across to the Italian Riviera. 'We went into this tiny café in San Remo and I ordered spaghetti bolognaise. And I started chopping up the spaghetti into bitesized pieces with a spoon and fork because I didn't know how to eat it. Oh, the waiter was horrified! He shot up to me, he picked up my spoon and fork, he twisted it round and he fed me. Every time I opened my mouth he'd stuff another load in and he was doing it with such charm I couldn't stop him. Anyway I couldn't digest it and I finished up going outside and I was terribly sick.'

Above: Eating al fresco in Florence – foreign food was a new and alarming experience for many British tourists, but would eventually have a significant effect on eating habits back home.

After the initial trauma many fell in love with continental cuisine and brought back a taste for garlic, olive oil and Mediterranean dishes that would long outlive their holidays, helping to change cooking and eating habits at home. They brought a whole new style back to the British suburbs, a style epitomised by the food writer Elizabeth David whose books (including *Mediterranean Food* and *French Country Cooking*)

THE LURE OF THE MEDITERRANEAN

revolutionised middle-class cuisine.

Pamela Woodland remembers her 1958 holiday to France as a real turning point. 'At breakfast time we went into this restaurant and in front of me was a bowl and I thought I wonder if it'll be Kellogg's cornflakes or Rice Krispies, that's how blinkered I was. In France a bowl at breakfast time is for coffee and along came the waitress with a big jug and she poured lots of coffee into this bowl, but when I came to pick it up I couldn't find the handle. I looked around to see what everyone else was doing and they were just picking it up with both hands and putting it to their lips. So that's how I learnt how to drink French coffee out of a French bowl. As soon as we came back to England I bought some bowls and we did it at home. Then there was the lovely French bread, the croissants, the beef tomatoes, the omelettes, all these things were virtually unknown in England and we learnt about them and started buying them and eating them at home.'

The British abroad also began to develop a taste for wine. But for some it was a sharp learning curve. Richard and Dorothy Isles arrived on the Italian Riviera totally innocent about the drinking habits of the locals. 'We were very thirsty and desperate for something to drink in San Remo,' says Richard. 'We noticed the locals were drinking this red liquid from ordinary pop bottles so we went into a shop and bought three of them. We took it back to the car and drank it as if it was Tizer. Well, I'm afraid it turned out to be red chianti and we both got so drunk. It was terrible, we were unconscious for a day and a half in our tent. We were teetotal so we didn't know anything about drink.'

Excessive drinking in the hot Mediterranean had a similarly disastrous effect on George Field's second honeymoon in 1948. 'We went to Monte Carlo because we'd been married during the war and hadn't been able to have a honeymoon, so I vowed we'd go there when it was all over. This was what I thought to be the most glamorous and romantic place in the world. We'd booked into one of the top hotels with a complete suite looking right across the harbour. We put the children to bed and we dressed up for dinner and we had all these waiters hovering over us, so I ordered a bottle of champagne because it was a special occasion.

'I'd forgotten that my wife didn't really drink and she was drinking this champagne like lemonade. The waiter kept filling her glass and she started giggling and the waiters had to help her to her feet after the meal. Anyway, I'd ordered another bottle of champagne to be taken up to our balcony and with the moon shining across the water this was going to be so romantic, I was looking forward to a night of passion. Of course, I had to put her to bed and she passed out, and I spent the night by myself drinking champagne on the balcony looking at all the yachts.'

One thing that didn't disappoint was the Mediterranean itself. Many remember being struck by their first sight and swim in a sea so different to anything they'd known back home. 'My first view of the Mediterranean I thought it was heaven, it was so blue, nothing like the grey sea we had at home,' remembers Dorothy Isles. 'I couldn't wait to get in and have a swim, it was so tempting, it almost said, "Come on

Top: One of the original Thomas Cook travellers' cheques.

Above: The beach scene, and the sunshine, abroad differed greatly from that back home and early British tourists often suffered from the effects of sunstroke and burning.

in, I've been waiting for you." So I took the lilo which was our bed and floated on it. I'd never been in a sea that was so warm and you could see the bottom, you could see the fish, it was wonderful.'

The British, however, weren't well equipped for fun on the Mediterranean. Old habits died hard and the tradition of dressing up to go down to the beach was still alive and well among some of the pioneer tourists in the South of France. 'I always wore a shirt and tie, coat, hat, shoes and socks when I went onto the beach,' recalls Chris Fawcett, a former sales representative for a biscuit company from Colne in Lancashire. 'We thought we were dressing correctly, that was what we had got used to in England. And I'd never come across temperatures so hot but I still kept my jacket

and tie on all the time. The afternoons were particularly hot and we couldn't understand why all the continentals had gone in and the sun loungers were empty. We'd just stay out there in the sun, all dressed up. I think one reason we stayed out was because you wanted your money's worth.'

The sophisticated women of the Riviera were pioneering a new fashion in swimwear – the bikini, named after Bikini Atoll in the Pacific where the US undertook nuclear testing in 1946. The designer, Louis Réard, created the bikini which was so small that Parisian models refused to wear it on the catwalk and several countries including Spain, Italy and Portugal banned it. But the ladies of the Cote d'Azur instantly

Above: The Brits were no strangers to crowded beaches and would certainly have felt at home here at Nice in 1963.

97

THE LURE OF THE MEDITERRANEAN

adopted it, scandalising the rest of the world. Kathy Vyse, a typist from Swansea, went to the Riviera in search of glamour in 1952 but felt drab in comparison to the women she found there. 'The French girls all seemed so sexy with their bikinis and so tanned, we just felt naive and unattractive. We were dressed too formally with our long posh dresses and little white gloves.'

Even fashion-conscious young British women, more adventurous in their beachwear, were easily outshone by their Riviera rivals – and could end up with an inferiority

complex. Margaret Maudsley, then the wife of a Bradford businessman, remembers her first day on the beach at Monte Carlo in the summer of 1958. 'I'd imagined I was the height of fashion with my one-piece white swimsuit with embroidered guitars, then I saw all these beautiful girls in bikinis. When they weren't on the beach they were walking round town with their high-heeled shoes and little pink poodles and a big pink hat. My husband's mouth dropped, he loved it, he thought it was Christmas and Easter all come at once. He was nearly bumping into lampposts, he couldn't take his eyes off these girls. But I was so pale, I was like a milk bottle going sour and my swimsuit looked so old-fashioned. My husband wanted me to buy a bikini, but no, I'd have had to run to the water with a towel wrapped around me if I was wearing one, so

Above: Away from the crowded beaches, the Riviera lifestyle was still completely alien to most British tourists.

I just stood around in my swimsuit admiring these beautiful bronzed women.'

Pamela Woodland was one of the few British holidaymakers who took the plunge and bought a bikini. 'I'd first gone down to the beach in navy blue college shorts down to my knees, I looked every inch, I realise now, a very prim English schoolmistress. And my husband had his tennis shorts on, down to his knees. When we arrived at the beach we looked on in amazement, we'd never seen anything like it in our lives. We'd been to Brighton and Bournemouth, but no beach was like this. We looked so ridiculous so we decided to go to a boutique and buy some new swimming costumes. I bought a red two piece with white spots, it was so short, I'd never worn anything as short as that showing all that leg and I wore that outfit all holiday and I wore it when I got back to England until it dropped to bits.'

Most shocking and disturbing of all to the early British tourists in the South of France was the prevalence of naturism on the beaches. Though attracted by the Riviera's erotic and sensuous image, and the promise of seeing topless or naked bathers, very few British tourists were prepared to entertain the idea of taking their own clothes off. The Cote d'Azur had in fact long been popular among naturists, many of whom travelled south from Germany. In 1963 the French government decided to make money out of this trend by endorsing the development of the world's first naturist resort at Cap d'Agde. Within 15 years it was growing rapidly, providing weekly accommodation for 20,000 nude holidaymakers and boasting its own naturist restaurants, supermarkets and banks. By 1978 it was estimated that 15 million Europeans went naked on holiday either to a naturist resort or to a topless beach, of which there were now many in the South of France. The Brits who were holidaying there were now much more likely to throw off their inhibitions and their clothes and join in. This was one of the effects of new liberal attitudes and the sexual revolution of the 60s and 70s. But most did not go with the intention of going naked – they stumbled across naturism by accident.

Above: Pamela Woodland – ultimately even the bikini had to go.

Pamela Woodland had by now grown to love the Mediterranean and was holidaying on the Riviera with her husband in the late 1970s. 'We came across a naturist beach, completely by accident. We saw the sign for it and I looked at my husband and he looked at me and he said, "I'm prepared to," and I said, "Well so am I." So he said, "Let's do it." He took off his trunks and I took off my cozzie. It was the very first time we'd bared ourselves in public. We stepped onto the beach and we were very, very self-conscious thinking people were looking at us. But we soon realised that we might as well have been invisible because nobody was taking a scrap of interest in us at all. And very soon I actually forgot I had a body, because the only time you feel you have a body is when you've got something on, because something's tight or something's itching or something's touching. It was a wonderful freedom, we found an empty dune and lay down together and I said to my husband this is absolutely fantastic. Our inhibitions were gone. We were converted to naturism of that kind – the sun, the sea, the sand, on a beautiful clean beach, with like-minded people.'

Most British naturists, like Pamela and her husband, did not publicise their new hobby. There were only a handful of naturist beaches in Britain and there was still a stigma surrounding the subject. Some feared for their jobs if they revealed that they

THE LURE OF THE MEDITERRANEAN

were naturists, so they kept it a private affair, largely restricted to summer holidays abroad. Mike McGregor was different. A successful businessman, he became one of the key exponents of the British naturist movement, starting his own magazine. He too had been converted by accident on a holiday to the South of France with his wife and children in 1975. 'By chance we came to this naturist beach and there were two or three hundred people and none of them had a stitch of clothing on. So I thought, "Are we going to sit here amongst all these naked people with our costumes on?" It was a bit embarrassing, then my wife said, "Blow this," and whipped her bikini off. I thought, "Oh my God, I've got to do the same," which I did. In the first place I felt naughty, you're laying there exposed and you're disobeying laws you've been brought up to respect. Of course, part of you feels good, because it's fun to be naughty, then I went to have a swim and it was very sensuous having nothing on. And when I came back to lie on my towel I felt a real peace, a wonderful feeling of ambience and togetherness with everyone else on the beach. It happened very quickly but I felt a different person, I felt so relaxed. And that experience changed my life. It became like a religion for me, I wanted to tell everybody about it, to convert them, to let them know how great it was and what they were missing.'

The prevalence of naturism in the South of France has never dented its exclusive and stylish image, or reduced its attraction for British tourists who consider themselves rather more discerning than most. The Cote d'Azur succeeded in retaining its upmarket image in an age of mass tourism. This allure partly stemmed from the continued presence of the rich and famous. The Riviera was immensely fashionable throughout the 1960s, 70s and 80s. Most glamorous of all was St Tropez, where Mick Jagger chose to wed Bianca at the luxurious Byblos Hotel, hounded by the world's paparazzi and where the now legendary Brigitte Bardot made her home. The South of France retained its more exclusive patronage with the development of luxury villas and apartments, but as millions flocked there every summer, the rapid commercialisation began to kill some of its charm and romance. Almost every inch of the coastline was built on, vast marinas were constructed, the beaches became terribly overcrowded, the coast roads suffered from high-season gridlock and parking at the resorts was a nightmare. All this did not deter Arab oil sheiks, millionaires, wealthy boat owners, rock stars, models and aspiring socialites, for whom the Riviera remained a mecca throughout the century.

From the late 1980s onwards, however, in reaction to the commercialised free-for-all on the coast, there was a movement away from the sea and towards the rural beauty of the unspoilt, peaceful and remote areas inland. Provence, with its traditional farmhouses and foods became a new, highly fashionable holiday attraction with British

Above: The 1980s saw a movement away from the overcrowded, built-up coastal areas of the Riviera, to inland beauty spots such as Provence.

holidaymakers renting *gites*. Its popularity was boosted by Peter Mayle's bestselling book *A Year in Provence*, which charted how he and his wife bought a 200-year-old farmhouse in the Lubéron and began a new life, mastering the Provençal accent, surviving the ineptitude of local builders, coping with the hilarious curiosities of French rural life and enjoying a host of traditional gastronomic delights. A new type of British holidaymaker came into existence – the 'affluent peasant' who envied the slow pace of life in the Mediterranean and sought to escape the stresses of the ratrace by spending their time off playing at being a peasant, staying in ramshackle farmhouses, preparing local foods and indulging in wine and siestas. By the 1990s a farmhouse holiday surrounded by the ancient vineyards and churches of Provence had become far more fashionable than an expensive apartment overlooking a crowded Mediterranean beach. While holidaymakers deserted the French Riviera in favour of its beautiful hinterland, a similar pattern emerged along the coast where the Italian Riviera came to be overshadowed by the new fashionability of Tuscany. The British went in search of *la dolce vita* following the olive oil trail away from the coast, enchanted by rustic recipes, cypress-dotted hills and historic farmhouses, preferably with swimming pools. They eulogised the wines, the vineyards and the traditional way of life on the 200,000 isolated farms in what came to be dubbed 'Chiantishire.'

The influence of these Mediterranean holidays on British life was immense and helped promote a social revolution in our eating and drinking habits. Returning holidaymakers wanted to bring back 'the good life'. Britons adopted the continental habit of eating out regularly and started frequenting French bistros and Italian trattorias or pizzerias. Consumption of wine increased 250 per cent between 1960 and 1980 and continental-style cafés arrived on British high streets. In the home, French country furniture came to Britain via Habitat and a fashion for quarry tiles was also inspired by travels in the Mediterranean.

The bulk of British holidaymakers who came under the spell of the South of France and Italy were overwhelmingly the more aspirational and adventurous middle classes. They were following in the footsteps of the jetsetters, the elite, the chic trend-setters and the creative set. They wanted individual holidays with style, holidays with cultural clout, fashionable and a bit exclusive. They didn't mind roughing it but they most definitely did not want to mix with the kiss-me-quick brigade. To the great relief of British devotees of the Cote d'Azur and Tuscany, there was never a mass invasion of holidaymakers from downtown, working-class areas. They were attracted elsewhere, so much so that by the late 1990s only one in 20 British holidaymakers were heading for France and Italy. The summer second home of the vast majority of British tourists from the 1960s onwards would overwhelmingly be Spain – on a package holiday.

Top: Tuscany became the Italian equivalent of Provence and was nicknamed Chiantishire due to the influx of Brits to the simple, isolated farmhouses . . .

Above: . . . complete with swimming pools.

THE PACKAGE HOLIDAY EXPLOSION

Irene Jackson, a young clerk from Burnley, first went abroad in 1967 on a package holiday. It was an experience she will never forget. 'Stepping off the plane at Ibiza airport was incredible. The doors opened, the heat flooded in and the smell of musk and pine mixed with cigar smoke. The airport building was just a large cabin with a straw roof, like something out of *Robinson Crusoe*. Unbelievable. Coming from a grey northern mill town, you can imagine when we saw all the lovely white painted houses with geraniums growing from the balconies, we felt we were in another world.'

From the 60s onwards there was a revolution in the holiday habits of the British. They began to go abroad in their millions on package holidays which offered an all-in deal of air travel, accommodation, meals and transit costs for one price. Pioneered by British tour operators, the package holiday brought a new world of exotic beaches and warm waters within the reach of the majority of the population. They offered direct, hermetically sealed routes to beachside hotels, involving minimal contact with foreigners, an idea which especially appealed to British holidaymakers who, at the time, couldn't speak any other languages and were suspicious of foreign foods. To begin with, the tourists were mostly middle class, but as the holidays became cheaper, most of those flying off to faraway destinations were drawn from the nation's working classes, people who had rarely ventured overseas – except when called upon to fight for their country in two world wars. They were lured first to Spain, the Balearics, the Canary Islands, then later to Greece, North Africa and Florida by the promise of sun, sea, sand and sex. The package holiday abroad came to replace the seaside holiday at home as the number one choice of the British on holiday.

In previous decades a foreign holiday for families who worked in factories, mills and mines was about as likely as a trip to the moon. Their mass migration abroad every summer was what was so new and startling about the boom in package holidays. But, almost from the beginning, their holidays on the Costas were surrounded by controversy. They were much maligned, the butt of snobbish comment which deemed them to be tasteless, narrow-minded, jingoistic, violent, promiscuous and

Left: An early advertisement for Thomas Cook's 'Air Tours Abroad' from 1950.

Opposite top: Majorca was one of the first Spanish islands to be targetted as a package holiday destination by the expanding British travel industry.

Opposite bottom: Water sports and beach activities like this 'Banana Boat' ride added to the 'family fun in the sun' appeal of Spanish beaches.

Below: Package holiday mass tourism turned the popular pastime of shopping for souvenirs into a whole new industry.

prejudiced, bringing Britain's good name abroad into disrepute. The budget tour operators who carried them also became a national joke, frequently going bust or serving up holidays from hell. The reality behind the many myths of the Brits abroad was far more complex and intriguing. One thing is clear, however, the first step they took on foreign soil often felt incredibly exciting – a huge liberation. According to Irene Jackson, 'The Spanish girls had bare legs; at home we wouldn't have dreamt of going without stockings, suspenders and stilettos. Not for long! Off came the stockings, we bought flip flops and shortened our skirts. Men in England were still wearing suits and shirts and ties, but on Ibiza it was colourful, open necked shirts, flared trousers and lovely tanned arms. Alcohol was very cheap and we would drink Cuba Libres until midnight. At home, women weren't even supposed to go in pubs. This was a life you could never even dream existed.'

The man who invented the first package holidays, and with it modern tourism, was Thomas Cook, a Baptist temperance campaigner from Market Harborough. In 1841 he

organised a mass railway excursion from Leicester to nearby Loughborough, not to make money, but to create a popular diversion from the evils of the public house. Encouraged by the success of this trip he went on to organise commercial tours to more and more distant destinations, using new rail, road and sea links to create a travel empire that, by the last decades of the 19th century, extended all over the world. There were Cook's tours to Paris, Pompeii and Palestine, many of them following the trail set by the Grand Tour, 100 years before. The tickets for foreign holidays, however, which generally included all transport and accommodation costs, were prohibitively expensive for the majority of the population. There were some attempts to make holidays abroad accessible to a wider public. Organisations like the Workers Travel Association – an offshoot of the trade union movement – and the Holiday Fellowship sold working-class holidays for an average week's wage, but their healthy, self-improving walking holidays in places like Switzerland never had mass appeal.

The provision of cheap air travel after World War II proved to be the turning point in the development of the modern package holiday. Until then travel by rail, road and sea was costly and immensely time-consuming. Although there was a growing demand for holidays abroad and surplus aircraft left over after the war as well as trained pilots to fly them, cheap air travel was slow to develop. The main reason was that the two national airlines British European Airways (BEA) and British Overseas Airways Corporation (BOAC) enjoyed a government-backed monopoly and were determined to stop any rival that undercut their prices on the main routes. The man who first cracked the scheduled airline's monopoly was a Reuters journalist, Vladimir Raitz. He and his tour company Horizon Holidays are acknowledged to be the trailblazers of the modern package holiday. In 1949 he went on holiday to Corsica, where he stayed at a makeshift holiday camp owned by friends and comprising US army surplus tents. When he left, his friends asked him to get together more clients for the following year. Considering that all but the most intrepid travellers would be put off by a 48-hour land and sea journey, he decided to charter a plane, and for £305 he secured an old American forces Dakota converted to take 32 passengers. 'I had to get permission from the Ministry of Transport and from British European Airways to fly it to Corsica. They were reluctant to give it because it would interfere with the BEA monopoly. Finally, after months of negotiations, just before Easter of 1950 we got it, but there was a condition – the only people that we could transport were students and teachers. Why

Above: Thomas Cook's monthly Traveller's Gazette magazine from 1903.

Above left: A £10 Thomas Cook 'Circular Note' traveller's cheque from 1874.

Opposite: Thomas Cook (1808-1892) founder of the travel empire.

THE PACKAGE HOLIDAY EXPLOSION

students and teachers I have never been able to discover. I remember one plane where the only passengers going out were two nuns. I declared them in the student category, perhaps they were novice, student nuns!'

These first flights of students and teachers proved to be a major turning point in the development of cheap, modern holidays by air. Undeterred, Raitz advertised in the Nursing Mirror and the New Statesman. *Holidaymakers live in large tents fitted with beds and mattresses. Meals are taken out of doors. English visitors will be pleased to find they are served twice daily with a meat dish.*" Over the first season he sold just over 300 holidays. The complete package cost £32 10s (equivalent to around £660 today) at a time when just a scheduled flight to Nice with BEA cost £70 (equivalent to over £1200).

Above: The introduction of jet aircraft like the Boeing 707 meant that more passengers could be carried, driving prices down.

One of the teachers to fly out on an early Horizon holiday to Corsica was Pamela Woodland. 'We read about this package tour to Corsica. For under £50 you were taken from London by plane to Corsica, full board, for two weeks, and you were brought back by plane to London. It was fantastic value for what it included and we said, "Let's go for it." I had always wanted to fly since the age of seven, so it was like a dream come true. We went from Stansted to Lyon where we stopped for refuelling, and then to Calvi. It was so exciting, I couldn't believe I was doing it.'

In the following years, sales of Horizon Holidays steadily increased, but during the 1950s there were still few airports to serve the developing tourist resorts and the one in Calvi was barely built. Patricia Baker recalls flying there in 1955. 'As we came in to land we all stood up and looked out of the windows. We weren't strapped in and what we saw was not a runway but a rough track in a field with blocks of stone on it that the pilot seemed to have to avoid. It was odd but I didn't know any better as it was my first flight.'

Air travel in the early days of charter flights was very different to today. The aircraft were much slower, they needed regular stops for refuelling and the cabins were unpressurised. As a result, they flew at low altitudes making them more vulnerable to turbulence and bad weather conditions. 'The passengers were thrown about much more in those days,' says Alan Treweke, another early passenger on Horizon Holidays flights. 'Almost everyone ended up vomiting and there were also lots of nosebleeds.'

Chris Fawcett recalls the atmosphere of terror on some of these early tourist flights. 'We went in an old wartime Dakota that had patched up bullet holes. When we saw it we were all a bit scared, but we'd paid our £22 for the holiday and didn't want to lose it. As the plane started up, there was a terrible noise because it wasn't insulated; it was only the shell and sackcloth. And when we took off it went very cold. I wanted to go to the toilet but you couldn't because there wasn't one. There was a policeman next to me and I said, "I wish we hadn't come on this, I wish I'd paid a bit extra and gone on a better plane." It got worse because we hit turbulence. Well, we didn't know what turbulence was, we didn't know what to expect and the plane went up, it went down, it went sideways, it dipped, we thought we were about to die. There were some old ladies sitting at the back of the plane and they started singing *Abide With Me* to keep everyone's spirits up.'

Many of the planes used were old, wartime, piston-engined aircraft bought at knockdown prices. They were not only uncomfortable, some were positively dangerous. The risks taken by the pioneering passengers are vividly recalled by Vincent Cobb, former manager of the early package tour operator Gaytours of Blackpool – so named

Above: Stylish Thomas Cook advertisement from 1950.

THE PACKAGE HOLIDAY EXPLOSION

before the gay liberation movement of the 60s changed the meaning of the word forever. 'I used to fly on the planes, that was part of my job to organise everything in the resorts we went to and the passengers had no idea of the danger they were in. The safety standards were very low and planes were falling out of the sky left, right and centre. The aircraft were old DC3s and DC4s, and very often they just weren't up to the job of landing in difficult conditions. One blew up in Majorca. I was on so many trips where we crash-landed or overshot the runway. Once it happened three times in a row on consecutive flights. I remember one very sad occasion when we undershot the landing at Ibiza and ended up in the sea, everyone just about got out safely, then an elderly woman insisted on going back to get her bag. She drowned. Sometimes passengers who'd had bad experiences would refuse to get on the plane to come home.'

Surprisingly – and thankfully – there were very few major British air disasters involving charter flights, but many near misses. One occurred on 9th October 1960 when a Hermes airliner overshot the runway at Southend airport and crashed onto the main railway line to London. Two minutes previously a train had passed by carrying 500 passengers. Miraculously, there were no deaths and only 7 of those on board were slightly injured. One of the passengers was Dorothy Bax. 'We were on our way home from our first holiday abroad. It was raining very hard on the approach and was very bumpy. I suddenly saw grass outside the window, then everything happened at once. All the luggage compartments opened and showered bags down onto us and we stopped at a funny angle. We were lucky that the plane had backward facing seats, that must have saved lives. You didn't have time to be frightened. When we got home the first thing my father said was, "Bad accident at Southend airport, did you see anything?" It didn't put me off flying, I've flown thousands of miles since and I always say, it can never happen twice.'

Stoic British passengers weren't going to let a few air scares deter them from their holidays abroad and the demand for package holidays continued unabated. We were an air-minded nation in the 1950s, perhaps a legacy of the glorious role played by the RAF in the Battle of Britain and the pivotal importance of air power in the winning World War II. There were a growing number of entrepreneurs who realised there were profits to be made by combining two of the nation's great loves – aeroplanes and holidays. More and more private airlines and tour operators were formed, flying from minor airports such as Lydd, Southend and Gatwick. But there was still official resistance and the privateers were only allowed to run occasional flights. Route applications were regularly turned down, often at the last minute, so that companies were frequently forced to print their programmes before knowing whether or not they really would be able to offer a particular destination. In the late 1950s, Harold Bamberg, who had begun operating air cruises around the

Calvi
CORSICA

*Information to
make your stay in Calvi
more enjoyable*

FINDING OUT may be fun but during a short holiday it can mean a waste of time and possibly missing things. Here is all the information you will normally need. Please read it and do not forget to look up corrections and additions on Horizon Holidays Notice Boards in the Hotels and in the Chalets Tamaris.

HORIZON HOLIDAYS LTD

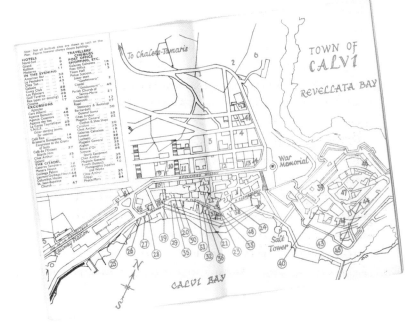

Mediterranean, decided to do battle with the state carriers. Linking up with travel agent Peter Cadbury, owner of Sir Henry Lunn Ltd, he began to apply not simply for routes, but for routes linked to low cost, all-in package holidays. Convincing the authorities that he was providing low cost travel for people who could never have afforded BEA and BOAC fares, he was granted permission to fly to Viareggio, a minor airport on the Tuscan coast of Italy. For his next destination, Bamberg selected a little known, undeveloped Spanish island in the Balearic Sea – Majorca. The flight took four and a half hours and the holiday cost almost £40, inclusive, for two weeks.

By this time, BEA itself was beginning to join the holiday game. It introduced cheaper 'tourist' class fares on its routes and in 1957 launched flights between London and the Spanish city of Valencia. On 4th May, BEA made its maiden flight to Valencia. On board were 18 holidaymakers and 10 journalists, invited by BEA to come and discover the 'Costa Blanca.' The name, locals read with bemusement in their local paper, was a British invention. For some reason BEA had named the coast after a hotel called the Costablanca. Their intervention in the holiday travel business coincided with the introduction of big commercial jet aircraft like the Boeing 707. With capacity for 189 passengers, jets offered twice as many seats as their predecessors, so there was a big incentive to increase demand. As the main flag-carrying airlines bought new jet aircraft, so their old ones were discarded at bargain prices, in turn encouraging the growth of charter flights.

Mainland Spain was about to be discovered by the modern package holiday business. At the time it was one of the poor men of Europe and the Franco dictatorship was deeply suspicious of foreigners, even happy to keep them out. Then, in the late 1950s Franco embarked on a bold policy to improve the nation's standard of living by encouraging mass tourism as a way of attracting much needed foreign currency. Tourist offices were set up all over Europe and a marketing campaign was launched, designed to lure people away from the French and Italian Rivieras. The Balearics, particularly Majorca and Ibiza, were used along with the Costas as testing grounds for a new kind of Mediterranean holiday. Fishing villages were transformed into concrete resorts, with an abundance of Miami-style high rise hotels. The government gave generous subsidies for hotel building and nobody bothered much about building and planning regulations. In 1957 the little fishing village of Benidorm, south of Valencia, had just 2,726 inhabitants. They made their living fishing, farming, weaving donkey panniers from esparto grass and sewing canvas sails. Every summer its beaches attracted only a handful of well-heeled holidaymakers to its three small hotels and eight boarding houses. Its roads were unpaved and it had barely any services. Two

Above: British airports like Gatwick expanded rapidly to cope with the increased demand from sunseekers.

THE PACKAGE HOLIDAY EXPLOSION

years later Benidorm had 34 hotels, four cinemas, boutiques selling French perfumes and Swiss watches, and fashion shows at the hotels. During August and September there were over 30,000 visitors and, according to the local paper, sports cars had taken the place of donkeys in the streets. By 1960, 300 new buildings had been completed, including 30 blocks of flats. Some locals complained that streets were blocked by building sites, café tables and cinema queues. Most, however, were only too pleased to welcome tourism. Land had increased at least a hundredfold in value, while prime seafront plots were fetching up to a thousand times the expected price. There was plenty of work, and many fishermen and farmers found jobs in the building trade, or as restaurant or hotel staff.

One of Franco's most curious legacies to Spain has been as the forefather of the modern pleasure-seeking holiday industry, but he cast a long shadow over early visitors to Spanish resorts. In 1956 the Browns of Nottingham holidayed in Tossa del Mar near Barcelona. According to George Brown, 'There were a lot of guards patrolling up and down the beach. You couldn't walk off the beach with your shoulders uncovered or a guard would stop you. There were strict codes of behaviour. We went to a bar one night and I was dancing with my arms around my wife when suddenly the police appeared, stopped the music and made me put my arms around her waist in the "proper dancing position."'

Brits abroad had to be very careful about any public show of affection. Until the late 1960s Spain was still a deeply conservative country with ultra-orthodox Catholic values. The police enforced 'public morals' of a kind that seemed very old fashioned to British visitors. Women who wore bikinis on the beach could be arrested for public indecency. In 1962 a law was passed forbidding anyone over the age of fourteen from wearing swimming costumes anywhere except on the beach or by a swimming pool.

'We had to put all our clothes back on just to get from the beach, over the road, to our hotel,' says Joan Mitchell, who visited Majorca in the early 60s. 'You daren't not do it because the police were on the beaches and there could be a very unpleasant scene.'

By law tourists were expected to behave according to the 'traditional good customs of Spain,' and if they didn't, managers of hotels, bars and nightclubs had the right to refuse entry and call the police. Until 1967 kissing in public was considered 'contrary to morals and decent behaviour,' and couples caught in the act could be fined anything from 125 to 1,000 pesetas. With the mass influx of tourists from the 60s onwards, Spain needed to court the holidaymakers in the interests of hard cash. As a result the authorities began turning a blind eye to what they considered to be the indiscreet behaviour of the Brits abroad. The strict rules governing public behaviour were relaxed

Above: The ubiquitous toy donkey became a much-desired souvenir for kids on a Spanish holiday.

Opposite: 1960 saw the start of the building developments which would turn Spain's sleepy fishing villages into forests of high-rise concrete.

and then abolished with the democratisation after Franco's death in 1975. By the early 80s topless bathing was commonplace on the Costas, an extraordinary change from the Victorian style regulations in force just 20 years earlier.

Throughout the early 1960s, very few British working class families could afford to go on a package holiday abroad. They were largely the preserve of the middle and lower middle classes.

THE PACKAGE HOLIDAY EXPLOSION

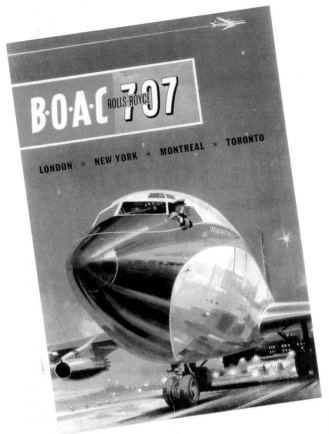

To encourage those of more modest means, some travel companies offered holidays on credit, but there were few takers – this was one branch of the 'never, never' which never took off. The person who initiated the quest to really cut the cost of holidays was Tom Gullick, an ex-navy officer, who started a small travel agency called H. Clarkson. He realised that there were vast numbers of people desperate for a foreign holiday if only it was cheap and easy enough. In 1965 he decided to take a chance with the Spanish summer holiday market. By negotiating rock bottom room rates from hoteliers, and deftly timetabling his charters, he managed to undercut his competitors by 20 to 30%. The season was a sell-out, and by the end of the decade Clarksons was the most successful tour operator in the country, sending millions of people abroad every year and accounting for 60% of Benidorm's trade. This was the beginning of vertical integration of the foreign holiday trade with tour operators like Clarksons building and buying hotels to cut out the middleman and reduce costs. At the same time from the late 60s onwards there was a rapid concentration of the industry and hundreds of smaller companies were swallowed up by a few big operators like Clarksons and the Thomson group. The consequence was that British tour operators were able to offer the cheapest holidays in Europe. In the early 1970s the lowest price for a two week package holiday to Spain in a one star hotel was around £20 (equivalent to around £220 today).

The new package holidays were offered all year round – as tour operators bought up airlines and hotels they needed to use them to maximum capacity – and the biggest bargains were often outside the main summer holiday season. This was how many less affluent people first went overseas, taking advantage of cut-price, out-of-season fares.

Most of those who went were couples or families, a change from the old tradition of whole communities holidaying together. Remarkably, however, the communal tradition survived in a diluted form as pensioner's groups and bowls clubs saved up to go away. It was almost as cheap – and a lot warmer – to spend a month or even the whole winter in Benidorm, rather than at home. The most extraordinary communal holidays abroad were those of the Blackpool hoteliers. When the season ended in October, half of Blackpool packed its bags and set off for a cheap holiday in the sun, coming home just in time for the upturn in trade at Christmas. Ironically, they were heading for the very resorts which were eroding the English seaside holiday – Benidorm, Majorca and the Canary Islands. In the 1970s, Pat Mancini was a Blackpool landlady. 'When the lights [illuminations] finished in October we all went away to Majorca. It was just like moving Blackpool over there. £72 full board for a month in a one star hotel. It was absolutely fabulous. You knew everybody, everywhere you went, "Hi, what you doing here?" "Saw Nellie at the airport." "When's your mum coming over?" and you knew everybody's business. It was like being in Blackpool except we had this wonderful sunshine. I mean, it was November and the main topic of conversation was, "Amazing sun isn't it? We couldn't do this is England."'

The package holiday industry was tapping into an almost insatiable demand for holidays abroad in the new, aspirational, affluent Britain of the 60s, 70s and 80s. The standard of living in Britain was – for the majority – steadily increasing and a holiday abroad began to feature highly among the most prized status symbols. Out of a range of consumer choices the British were consistently placing holidays high in their annual spending. Along with mortgage repayments and running a car, it became one of the most costly items in the family budget. As they saved up each year for the holiday of their dreams, one of the old items of expenditure to suffer most was gambling. Despite the legalisation of high

Below: Pat Mancini enjoying the attention of a Spanish waiter in Majorca.

THE PACKAGE HOLIDAY EXPLOSION

street betting shops in the 60s, the proportion of people's income spent on the dogs, the horses and the pools declined, just as holiday spending increased. The certainty of two weeks on a beach in Spain or the Greek Islands proved to be more attractive than the hit or miss chance of a small windfall at the bookies.

In the past, a holiday abroad had been almost unimaginable to most working class people; it was something they associated with film stars, jetsetters and the super rich. Now, with cheap package holidays and the low cost of living in countries like Spain, they felt like film stars themselves. In the 1950s Lola Smith had spent holidays working in the hopfields of Kent – by the late 60s she was jetting off to Ibiza. 'When we went to

Ibiza I couldn't even pronounce it. I was only ordinary, but when I got to the airport I thought, "I feel just like a film star," and I'm sure you acted as though you was something better than you was because you were going abroad. You never thought you were going to travel like this on a jet, you felt very important. And when you got there you loved the money, the pesetas, because with your money you could buy anything, it was all so cheap. You could get a big vodka and tonic for a shilling [five pence] and I think cigarettes were only one and six for twenty [seven and a half pence].'

Pat Mancini remembers, 'I just felt like I was really rich. It was only a cheap holiday, I know, in a one star hotel but because I'd never had holidays in the sun, I thought that was what the rich people did. I thought I was with the big money. When

Above: Irene Jackson and friends enjoying the nightlife of San Antonio in Ibiza in 1969.

114

you stood at the bar you felt as if you'd arrived. These people that were serving you looked at you maybe thinking you were upper class or something because you'd been able to come all that way and they'd probably never left their island, they'd been fishing all their lives. It made you feel good. And you had all those pesetas in your pocket and everything was cheap, the drinks were cheap, so your money lasted for ages. And I used to give them a tip, leave one or two pesetas and when you did that they'd ring the bell to mark it, well you felt really special then.'

As the holiday abroad became established as a source of prestige and glamour in the swinging 60s, holidaying in Britain came to be regarded as second rate. Some children were embarrassed that their parents weren't going abroad like their more fashionable classmates. In 1967 pester power led the Lentons from Wakefield to give up their annual British seaside holiday. Betty Lenton recalls, 'We'd always gone off in our lorry to the seaside but my eldest daughter Jane, she came home from school one day and said, "All my friends go abroad and I'm not going away in that wagon again, I want to go abroad." And she went on and on. So that's how we came to go to Ibiza.'

The massive increase in demand meant that tour operators could afford to charter much better aircraft. By the early 70s almost half of all charter fleets were jets, much faster, smoother and more comfortable than the old piston-engined planes that had dominated the trade ten years before. They also had a much greater range, allowing them to reach many more destinations without refuelling. But there was a new problem. To keep prices down, the jets were often timetabled for three return journeys a day to Spanish resorts like the Balearic Islands. With everything run on a shoestring budget, there was no leeway when things went wrong, as they frequently did. Long, nightmare delays at airports became the bane of the holidaymaker. 'I reckoned that if a flight was six hours late, that was good, but ten hour delays or longer were very common,' says Vincent Cobb, former managing director of Gaytours. 'One of my jobs was to try to placate the passengers but the

Below: Lola Smith – holidaying in Ibiza was vastly different to holidaying on the hop farms of Kent.

115

THE PACKAGE HOLIDAY EXPLOSION

communications to other countries were very primitive in those days and very often we just didn't know where the plane was or when it would arrive. Then when it came in it had to be turned round very quickly to go off again. When the passengers got angry, you'd usually find there would be a ringleader and one of our strategies was to get him and say, "There could be a problem with the plane but the captain says he's prepared to take the risk if you are, too." That always did the trick and they'd back off and sit down again.'

What was perhaps most extraordinary was the lack of formal complaints to tour operators during the early years of the package holiday industry. Although ABTA, the Association of British Travel Agents, had been set up to monitor the standards of operators and provide some machinery for complaints and compensation, few aggrieved holidaymakers seemed to take advantage of it. They often had no recognition of their rights and just took what happened in their stride as part of the adventure of holidaying abroad. Ruby Webster's first holiday abroad to Majorca in the early 70s was typical of such experiences. She travelled on a charter plane which hadn't been properly serviced or even repaired. 'I'd never been on a plane before when we went from Birmingham to Majorca. My husband and I were a bit afraid, but we sat back and when it took off, it really took your breath away. Then we levelled out and suddenly I could feel all this water coming down on my shoulder. I said to my

Above: Once new jet aircraft with sufficient range were in service, longer non-stop flights became prevalent and the Greek Islands fell to the onslaught of mass tourism.

116

husband. "Tom, it's raining." and he said, "Don't be silly, it doesn't rain in planes." Well, it must have been a leak from something above me. That was just the beginning though, the ashtray came off, then I pulled down the table to have a cup of tea and that came off in my hands. And finally a steward started wheeling an old fashioned trolley with the duty-frees that had two bicycle-like wheels at the front. As he was pushing it, one wheel came off and rolled down the aisle and my husband caught it. I said, "This is never right, this plane is falling to pieces as we're going along." I really thought I was going to die, I thought that was it. Of course we never complained, most people never dreamt of complaining in those days.'

The British, however, did become more savvy about their holidays abroad and as the complaints increased, so the tour operators were forced to deliver the travel arrangements, accommodation and beaches they advertised in their brochures. One significant factor in the raising of consumer awareness was the introduction of TV holiday programmes, first the BBC's weekly *Holiday* programme beginning in 1969, followed by ITV's *Wish You Were Here* in 1974. They – and related programmes – consistently put package holidays under the spotlight and acted as a watchdog for holidaymakers. There was no shortage of stories to probe. Unbuilt hotels, hotel complexes that were virtual building sites, substandard rooms, severe overcrowding and insanitary facilities were all regular features. As a whole new set of holiday resorts sprung up in Spain, the Balearics and the Canaries, holidaymakers were made aware that some of the beaches they were hoping to sunbathe on only existed in the pages of the brochures. They were manmade and hastily constructed, along with the hotels, with money obtained through advanced bookings. The following decades would see a tenfold increase in complaints to tour operators, making the holiday abroad one of the main areas for consumer criticism and dissatisfaction.

Above: Cheap drink in Mediterranean resorts was the downfall of many a fledgling tourist.

Yet despite all these disappointments and hazards, the British kept signing up for their package holidays in ever increasing numbers. Though television programmes highlighted some of the flaws of holidays abroad they were also a powerful advertisement, bringing their alluring pleasures to a mass audience on a regular basis. The trend was towards ever greater spending on holidays abroad. What drove the demand as much as anything else was the new fashion for a suntan. Britain became a nation of sun worshippers and a bronzed body became an essential prerequisite for anyone who wanted to show off their summer wardrobe and be seen to have sex appeal. Gone were the days of the pale English rose and parasols on the prom. Now, if you didn't have an all over tan, dark enough to convince everyone that you'd been abroad, you were considered sad and unfashionable. Tans were planned like military

THE PACKAGE HOLIDAY EXPLOSION

Above: Pat Mancini (centre) left her Blackpool guesthouse for a sunnier holiday in the Med.

operations and whole days or weeks would be spent on holiday nurturing the right shade of brown to come home with. A tanned look seemed to denote status, sex, money, sophistication and good health and it was a look most people of all ages wanted.

'It was a newish thing then to get a good suntan and it was very important to me,' say Cassie McConachy, who holidayed in Majorca in 1972. 'I can remember sitting on the plane thinking, "Oh, God, I hope it's really hot there," panicking in case it wasn't and when you got off the plane you'd be staring at the people going home to see how tanned they were, to check if it was going to be good. I wanted to be tanned all over and most of the time I just used to lay out in the sun, covered in olive oil and vinegar. When I was tanned it made me feel good when I got back to England and nobody else had one like I did, which was fantastic. You could have been in Majorca for a fortnight and you'd say you'd been to the Bahamas for a month, depending on how good your tan was. We were all in very short miniskirts then and the tan was great because then you didn't have to wear horrible tights; with bare legs you were sexier. That used to really give me a kick.'

Many wanted tans so badly that they suffered severe sunburn and sunstroke. In the late 1960s and 70s there was still little awareness of the dangers of rapid and excessive exposure to the sun's rays. The new generation of package holidaymakers, like Lola Smith from Bethnal Green, threw caution to the wind. 'Me and my husband, we just desperately wanted a great tan. We wanted friends back home to notice and say, "Oh, you've gone a lovely colour." On the first day we went down to the beach straight after breakfast and we laid there in the sun all day, in the water, out of the water. Well, the salt burns you shocking. We didn't realise that, we were just laying out there. When it was six o'clock we got up, we'd got sunstroke. We got upstairs to our room shivering and the next day we came out in blisters. That's when I became homesick, I felt so ill. The Spanish waiters said, "Oh, you should have covered yourself," They didn't go out in the sun, only mad dogs and Englishmen.'

Betty Lenton also suffered from sunstroke on her first holiday abroad to Ibiza in 1967. 'One of the big things for me about going abroad was to sunbathe, I loved to lay in the sun, so on our first holiday I was lying in the sun all day. I'd fallen asleep and my husband Ronnie had gone off sightseeing. When he came back I woke up and felt absolutely awful. I said, "Give me some orange juice, I'm gagging." I didn't realise I'd dehydrated and glug, glug, glug, down went the whole glass. We walked back to the hotel and I remember getting in the lift, but then I passed out. Ronnie says he dragged me out of the lift and I lay unconscious. He was terrified, he thought I was going to die so he started smack, smack, smacking my face. Then I had this awful feeling of coming back to consciousness and I said, "I don't know who that is smacking my face but I do wish they'd stop it." In fact I had sunstroke which was extremely dangerous. I've managed to do it twice since, but I'm learning before it completely wrinkles all my face!'

Below: The shallow shores and safe beaches of the Mediterranean were a vast adventure playground for kids.

THE PACKAGE HOLIDAY EXPLOSION

It was only in the 1990s, that sun worshippers became more aware of the serious, long-term damage they were inflicting upon themselves. Apart from prematurely wrinkled faces, thousands eventually suffered – or will suffer – from skin damage and cancers caused by unprotected exposure. Though skin cancer used to be one of the rarest of all cancers, its prevalence has rapidly increased in the past two decades. One of the sufferers is Shelagh Hartley from Devon. 'I was a sun worshipper from as long back as I can remember. I was regularly sunburnt and I had sunstroke twice. Then one day in 1984 I noticed a mole on my ankle. I tried to ignore it but it wouldn't go away and in three or four years it changed from being something small and brown to something black and disgusting. When I went to the doctor, I was sent straight to a consultant who diagnosed skin cancer and they removed the mole straight away. Since then I've had two more removed from my legs and there will be more.'

Along with the suntan, another great attraction of the package holiday abroad was alcohol. This was especially true of the new Spanish resorts where a favourable exchange rate and a low cost of living meant that drinks were two or three times cheaper than they were at home. The licensing hours were also much more relaxed than in Britain and from the 1970s onwards many bars were open much of the day and into the night. For some holidaymakers like Cassie McConachy in Majorca, the cheap drink was just too much of a temptation. 'I went there with every intention of having a really good look at Majorca but I never got any further than the swimming pool of the hotel. I was rat-arsed all the time, out of my face ninety nine and a quarter per cent of the time. There was all these dishy little waiters saying, "Would you like a drink senora?" I don't even remember eating a meal there. It was all sangria and bacardi. Everything was so cheap, it was unbelievable, and they didn't have proper measures, they just tipped a load of the bottle in. It was sheer gluttony. You'd start off gently in the morning with a small glass of sangria; then you might have a big jug of it; then you flaked out – that was handy to get your tan going – then you'd wake up in a bit of a stupor, have a swim to sober up a bit; then more drink as you got towards the evening. Everybody had this alcohol agenda. You'd drink so much at night it was difficult to get back up the stairs to your hotel room. You'd come down in the morning and there would still be people asleep by the pool on sun loungers, where they'd obviously given up trying to stagger back the night before.'

There were a few arrests as British holidaymakers were drunk and disorderly in the bars and on the streets of the new Spanish resorts. But as Spain became more liberal and more dependent on the tourist industry, the police turned a blind eye to the drunken revelries and even helpfully escorted paralytic Brits back to their hotels. Pat Mancini recalls her holidays to Majorca in the 1970s. 'Of course you got drunk, you were on holiday weren't you, what the heck, go with the flow. Once I was in a bar and I drank so much I didn't know what I was doing. I thought I was taken back to my hotel in a taxi. It turned out later it was a police car, I was in such a state. Another

Wish you were here! Camp de Mar, Majorca

Above: One way of demonstrating to friends and family that you could afford an expensive foreign holiday . . .

Opposite top: Greek island hopping on the local ferries meant a constant change of scenery, breathtaking views and plenty of fresh sea air.

Opposite bottom: Another way of showing off a successful holiday – go home with an impressive suntan.

night we went to this wine tasting thing
and they started pouring wine down me.
They had these jugs with long spouts and
you open your mouth and the wine comes
flowing in. I was getting drunk and they
wanted a volunteer for flamenco dancing,
so I was up with the maracas and clicking
my heels, I was a Spanish dancer.'

For some, drunkenness arose from a
complete innocence about the potency of
sangria, which some early package holiday
visitors to Spain mistook for a refreshing
non-alcoholic fruit drink. Betty Lenton
recalls, 'There was this fantastic local
drink in a big jug called sangria. We were
all hot and sticky so the whole family had
a glass and I said, "This is delicious." I
thought it was non-alcoholic, nobody told
us there was wine in it. I thought it was a
health drink and with all the fruit it could
do us nothing but good. So we ordered
another jug and I was encouraging the
children to drink it too, which they did.
Then we're sat in the dining room and
Richard, he'd be about eight or nine then,
he suddenly became very tired. His head

kept dropping onto the table and I kept saying "Sit up, don't show me up."
Anyway, we carried on and had our soup with more sangria, then Richard's
head went down bang, he was out like a light. Ronnie, my husband, had to
carry him out of the dining room in front of all those people and back to
the room. Of course, it was only then that I realised that my young son
was drunk.'

Another of the big attractions of a package holiday abroad, especially
for younger people, was the prospect of romance and sex. The endless
media coverage of Brits in Spanish resorts enjoying 'fun in the sun,'
suggested that this was something new and sensational. In fact, it was a
development of a summer seaside tradition in Britain, well established
during the first half of the century. The difference was that the sexual
behaviour was now more open and more adventurous than before.
Gangs of friends went to Benidorm in search of a good time and
sexual conquests, just as they had done in Blackpool in previous
generations. Cassie McConachy remembers, 'If you went with your
mates, you wouldn't mind having one night stands. We'd had
closeted upbringings most of us, but in the 60s and 70s we were
determined to make up for it and have a good time, enjoy ourselves
under any circumstances. The drink helped, it helped you lose

THE PACKAGE HOLIDAY EXPLOSION

your inhibitions. It didn't matter if it was a Spaniard, an American or a German. You probably wouldn't have been seen dead with them at home, because everyone would talk about you, but on a holiday abroad nobody cared, you could sort of step out of bed in the morning and say, "Thanks very much, bye." It was something totally different from your life at home and you didn't have any of the constraints of your family or your neighbours, it was freedom.'

Young, unmarried couples booked in for holidays at beachside hotels just as they had up to the 1950s in English seaside boarding houses but now there was less need for deceit and subterfuge. From the 60s onwards many lived together before marriage anyway, giving the holiday a different significance altogether. 'We'd always wanted to make love on a warm, secluded beach,' says Dave Parker, who went to Majorca in 1969. 'It wasn't the sort of thing we fancied doing in England because it was too cold, but on a Spanish island, yes.' Sex on the beach, though, wasn't on the minds of all British couples. When Cassie McConachy went away with a boyfriend, 'Sex was absolutely out of the question. Too itchy, too hot, my suntan burns, my stomach's dicky, you know. There was no point. You could do that at home.'

It was so hot many couples – married or not – spent most of their time sleeping, sunbathing and drinking. But for a few the sexual promises hinted at by the holiday brochures did come true. Pat Mancini and her husband worked hard, day and night, all through the summer season in their Blackpool boarding house. In Majorca, at last they had time for each other. 'We made love more on holiday, it was all part of the holiday. I mean you never had sex in the afternoon at home because you were baking or frying chips or something, but on holiday – bang, crash, wallop – you've got time for it. So it was in the afternoon and at night. When you'd arrived abroad with the heat, the wine, the atmosphere, it was like the first time all over again. You were more sensual, lying there in bed with no sheets and nothing on.'

What was genuinely new about the sexual behaviour of Brits abroad was the increasing interest in romances with young people from another country and another culture. Sometimes the relationships would be with Germans, Dutch and Scandinavians met in bars and on the beaches. This mixing of nationalities on holiday had been rare in the past. Even more common were romances with local men in Spain, the Greek Islands and elsewhere. For Irene Jackson, who went to Ibiza in 1967, there was a major cultural barrier to the holiday romance – garlic breath. 'It was terrible, we weren't used to garlic at all then, but the Spanish lads really stank of it. Me and my girlfriends bought a load of Strepsils and when we got off with the Spanish blokes at the discos we made them suck a Strepsil before we kissed them!'

The presence of thousands of sexually liberated women in search of romance and a good time was an amazing temptation and opportunity for young men whose own girlfriends were highly religious, chaperoned by parents and brought up to believe that

Above: Greek island 'boarding house' accommodation could be quite basic, although somewhat more picturesque than its Blackpool equivalent.

Opposite: Chris Hall and her Greek Adonis.

122

sex before marriage was a sin. The ideal of the virgin bride was still alive and well in southern Mediterranean countries where the Catholic and Greek Orthodox churches still wielded enormous power. Inevitably, most young men would bow to family and community pressure and marry a woman from their own locality, but before they settled down many wanted to enjoy a good time with the British beauties arriving on their doorstep. The young British women had no idea that in the long term their holiday romance was likely to be doomed. Chris Hall first went to Naxos on a package holiday as a 17-year-old in 1977. 'Going to Greece for the first time had a big impact on me, it was just like heaven on earth, the sea, the sand, the stars, the heat, the lemons growing on the trees and the good-looking men, every one of them looked tanned and beautifully groomed. Then I saw one that particularly caught my eye. I was sitting in a beachside disco and in walked this man, his head held high and drop dead gorgeous. I thought he was one of the Greek Gods, a lot better looking than the men you met at home. I instantly fell in love. Then, lo and behold, five minutes later he asked me to dance. I had no knowledge of the Greek language, but he did introduce himself and he asked me where I was from, so I told him, "Chris from Scotland," and he said, "Hello, I'm Adonis the butcher." And off we went to dance. They played George Benson's *The Greatest Love of All*, which has remained my favourite song, and I just stared into his eyes and thought, "Oh goodness, he is beautiful." We couldn't say much but we didn't really need words.

'He was the perfect gent on the first night, just took me for a stroll on the beach, but on the second night in the same place we got more romantic. There was a little tent in the sand dunes, just behind the disco and we went in and that's where we had sex and I lost my virginity. What could be more special than a little tent on a Greek island with the sound of waves lapping on the shore? When it came time for me to go home he gave me his address and we started to write to each other. I went back for three holidays running and each time it was as fantastic as the first time, then a friend of his offered me a job as an au pair. So, of course, I thought that was perfect, I handed in my notice at work, I

THE PACKAGE HOLIDAY EXPLOSION

left my job, my friends and my family to be there with him on the island. Everybody thinks that their holiday romance is the romance of their lives and that you're the only one. Well, very quickly I found out that I wasn't. There was a line of them arriving every summer on the ferry, a different one every few weeks, some British girls, some Germans. I came to realise that even the love letters he'd been sending to me at home weren't written by him, they were written by a friend and there were probably carbon copies all over the world! It was very foolish of me to believe it all in the first place. So he was just snatched from under my nose, and it was very upsetting. Most of the local boys married local girls then, their families didn't want them marrying a foreign girl and this is what Adonis eventually did.'

If romance was high on the agenda of early package holidaymakers, savouring the delights of foreign cuisine was definitely not. In the 60s and 70s Spanish and Greek island hotels were relatively inexperienced in catering for what were then the conservative tastes of the British abroad. Some, in all good faith, served up local dishes and were surprised and disappointed to find many of them remained uneaten. Irene Jackson recalls the Ibizan hotel food she tasted in 1967. 'It was strange. They'd bring soup which was like dishwater with noodles in. Then the next course they'd bring was green beans, nothing else on the dish but beans and then the next course was potatoes on their own, then meat, no sweets, no desserts. They hadn't heard of chips then. I think all I could eat was breakfast because that was like bread and jam.'

Lola Smith had a similar experience in Majorca around the same time. 'I couldn't eat the food. If you had soup there would be oil floating on it, it was just the way they cooked. I think we lived on chocolate and crisps.'

On one occasion Pat Mancini and her husband complained. 'This meal they brought out to us was rainbow trout and don't forget we'd never heard of rainbow trout then. Well my husband called the waiter and he said, "It's got its teeth in, its eyes in and it's looking at us!" Of course we'd never seen a fish with its teeth and eyes like that. So we sent for the restaurant manager and all he could say was, "Yes, sir, rainbow trout." And my husband said, "Get its hat and coat and I'll take it for a walk because everything else is on it." We never ate it and I just killed myself laughing.'

To please their customers, hotels began laying on English dishes, or what they imagined to be English dishes. 'They must have heard that English people like brussel sprouts because I remember this awful soup they used to make,' says Cassie McConachy. 'It was called brussel sprout soup, the mind boggles. The smell was disgusting. The taste was worse.' Some holidaymakers tried to educate the Spanish hoteliers in the finer points of English cooking, suggesting dishes that they would like and in a few cases going into the kitchens and showing them how to cook it.

Ruby Webster holidayed in Majorca in the early 1970s. 'I loved the Spanish people

Above: Eileen Cook (second from left) joining in the fun with some Greek dancers in 1973. She was less keen on the sheep's head soup.

they were so friendly but I didn't go much on the food. In the hotel the puddings weren't up to much so I said to the waiter, "Have you ever heard of rice pudding?" He said, "No, no, not rice in the pudding," and I said "Yes, yes, yes." "You come see my cook!" So he took me into the kitchens and I told them how to make it. We had rice pud every day after that and the English people loved it. It was proper old English cooking, because in Majorca they didn't know a lot about English cooking in those days.'

After a few years of trial and error many of the hotels in Spain and the Greek Islands were providing British favourites like roast beef, burgers and chips on their menus. All-in self-service buffets were also introduced. These were much more popular than the three or four course meals served by waiters, which many tourists had found so intimidating. The risk element was removed for less adventurous holidaymakers who could stick to familiar British food. But for those who ventured off the beaten track, away from the hotels and tourist centres there could still be a shock in store. Eileen Cook and her husband Arthur befriended a local family in Rhodes and were invited to spend the Greek Easter with them. 'They had this tradition where they killed a lamb the day before, got it on the spit for roasting and all the bits and pieces that were left, the sheep's head and its entrails, they made a big stew out of it. So we were in this Greek home and the hostess served up these big bowls of soup with all the entrails in to eat with black bread. It was quite an honour to be included as one of the family. But the smell was terrible and I thought, "Oh God, I can't eat that." I got one or two mouthfuls down to be polite then when she was out of the room I opened up my handbag and tipped it all in, then zipped my bag up. Well, how deceitful can you be? It was my own fault because when she came back in she took one look at my empty bowl and said, "Oh, you love it, have some more," so I finished up with another big bowl. And when we left my handbag was congealed with sheep entrails, rice, cigarettes, lipstick, powder, combs, it was disgusting. I had to throw it away.'

Perhaps the worst nightmare of those holidaying abroad was to end up in a war zone. This was a rare event in Europe as the continent enjoyed an unprecedented

THE PACKAGE HOLIDAY EXPLOSION

period of peace in the second half of the century. One of the worst episodes involving British tourists occurred in the summer of 1974 when Greece and Turkey waged war over sovereignty of the island of Cyprus. Over 6,000 would die in the conflict, among them scores of holidaymakers, trapped as the Turkish air force and navy launched its initial attacks on the coastal towns. One of the first targets was the holiday town of Famagusta where Barbara Trigg and her husband from Dursley in Gloucestershire were staying. 'The holiday was wonderful to begin with, for the first time in our lives we'd booked ourselves into a five star hotel, the Venus Beach in Famagusta. I'd taken all my best clothes and jewellery with me and my husband had a new cream suit. Then one day, everywhere we went there were Greeks crowding around radios. When we got back to the hotel everyone went mad, there was total bedlam. Some were for Makarios and some were against and people were firing guns into the air. This was on the Monday and there was a curfew until the Thursday. No one was allowed to leave the hotel, we wondered what the hell was going to happen. Then at five o'clock one morning the staff came round banging on our door, everyone had to get up because there were Turkish gunboats in the bay and the bombing had started. We had to get down to the ground floor as it was safer. There were lots of Greek soldiers driving around, shouting and making all the boys working in the hotel come out and join in the fighting. As I looked over the balcony I saw one young lad run towards the troops and as he got there he obviously changed his mind and turned to run back in. They just shot him dead in the back. I was really frightened.

Above: Tourist tastes have developed over the years. As well as the familiar watersports and beach life, they now have the confidence to want to hire a car and explore inland.

'There were four cars at the hotel and the receptionist directed us to drive towards a safe area. We dug out an old Union Jack and put it on the car and piled in and as we did a bomb dropped almost next to us. The noise was indescribable, I'll never forget it to this day. Then we went driving through the orange and lemon groves but we were stopped by Turkish troops. I was in shock, I couldn't believe this was really happening, it was like being in a film. This had started off as a holiday. But I clung on to this belief, they won't hurt us because we're British. We were lucky, they let us go on and we were the last car to get out. We finally got to the British base and they flew us home in an old troop carrier. By then the island was in flames. We'd had to leave all our luggage behind but we never got any compensation – the military even tried to charge us for the flight home.'

The number of holidaymakers caught up in war zones was relatively few but many more suffered from tour operators going bust. In the boom years of the 60s there was little official regulation and all that was needed to set up as a tour operator was a brochure, a shop and a telephone. For anyone with a little money and a lot of nerve, there was money to be made, and the fledgling industry attracted hordes of young pioneers with a sense of adventure and a willingness to chance it. Inevitably there were casualties. One of them was Fiesta Tours which collapsed in July 1964, leaving holidaymakers stranded at Perpignan airport. Even though Fiesta was not a member of ABTA, Harry Chandler flew out as a representative of the association to discover that the stranded passengers had turned the airport into a refugee camp. Chandler

flew some of them home using empty seats on his own charters, while ABTA persuaded most of the big travel operators to cover the cost of flying the rest of the Fiesta customers home and providing holidays for those who had lost their money.

It was hoped that the rapid concentration of the holiday industry into the hands of a few huge tour operators would offer greater protection for the holidaymaker, but that proved to be wishful thinking. In 1973, in protest against American support for Israel in the Arab-Israeli Yom Kippur war, the oil states of the Middle East increased their prices by 70 per cent. One of the effects was an economic crisis in Britain and the travel industry was the first to suffer. The next year the tour operators added surcharges to their holidays to cover increased fuel costs and bookings were down by a quarter. Many holidaymakers decided to stay in Britain that summer. It was the first serious downturn in the overseas holiday market for many years and in August the inevitable happened. Court Line, a huge conglomerate made up of over 100 shipping, aviation and leisure companies – including Clarksons which by then accounted for 25 per cent of the holiday market – collapsed. Customers who had paid, but not yet had their holiday, besieged Clarksons' offices. Compensation was slow in coming, leaving many dissatisfied. The more immediate problem was the repatriation of 35,000 stranded holidaymakers in a huge rescue campaign orchestrated through ABTA and with the assistance of the government.

THE PACKAGE HOLIDAY EXPLOSION

One of the unlucky holidaymakers was John Bond. Like many others travelling to the Greek Islands that August, he envisaged that the only possible problem on the holiday might be the disruption caused by the war in Cyprus. 'It was late August 1974 and I was going on holiday with my wife and some relatives to Corfu, travelling with Clarksons on board a Courtline flight. It got off to a bad start at Cardiff airport when the flight was delayed for 20 hours because of the war in the airspace around Cyprus. When we eventually took off the flight was uneventful until we were on our descent path, when over the P.A. system the pilot announced that Courtline-Clarkson had gone into liquidation. There was a ghastly silence, then uproar followed when we landed. The coach drivers were unhappy about payment if they took us to our hotel and the manager was none too happy to take us in as guests. The Clarksons reps worked hard to get the manager to take us on a day-to-day basis. But our first breakfast was a disaster because all the hotel catering staff had been commandeered for the war effort in Cyprus. Only old gardeners and labourers were left to do any cooking. So my wife together with some other guests organized a rota to provide meals.

'Every day was both an adventure and a worry. The Clarksons rep had no news of our possible return home. Our hotel was now dominated by the smell of Shepherds pie and Lancashire hotpot. On the last day of our holiday the rep told us that British Caledonian would take us back, but it flew to Gatwick, not Cardiff. Most of us didn't have enough money to get back to Cardiff so we shared out all the money we had. Looking back I think it brought back something of the wartime spirit of survival and camaraderie.' The Court Line failure was huge but it was far from being the only one. In the 18 months leading up to December 1974 18 ABTA tour operators and 17 agents collapsed.

In the 1980s and 90s the package holiday remained the holiday of choice for the vast majority of Britons travelling abroad. The number of holidays abroad taken more than doubled during this period, so that by 1999 more than 14 million people took an overseas package holiday. By this time 7 out of 10 Britons had taken a holiday abroad, whereas 50 years before just 200,000 people were crossing the Channel annually. One

Above: Freddie Laker took on the big boys of the aviation business just as Vladimir Raitz and Harold Bamberg had done before him and Richard Branson would do after him.

new trend was the development of long haul holidays to America, the Caribbean, Australia and the Far East, which by 1999 was accounting for one and a half million British holidays. The man who pioneered cheap flights to the United States was Freddie Laker with his walk-on, no frills 'Skytrain,' introduced in 1977. A ticket cost just £59, three times less than it cost to fly with any of the major airlines. Florida, the 'Sunshine State,' soon became the most popular destination for long haul Brits, as families flocked to join the forty million or more tourists per year who visited the string of new theme parks that came to dominate the Orlando landscape. Most popular of all was the ever-expanding Walt Disney World. First opened in 1971 it has since attracted five hundred million visitors, making it the biggest tourist attraction in the world.

Most Brits, however, continued to go to Spain which was the destination for almost half of those holidaying abroad. The Costas, the Balearic Islands and the Canaries still offered some of the cheapest and most accessible holidays in the sun and many Britons chose to settle in Spain for their retirement. The facilities provided were updated and improved from the 1980s onwards, the tackiest resorts benefiting from facelifts with new parks and seafront promenades. A number of the old one star skyscraper hotels built in the 60s were blown up and replaced with more attractive developments monitored by the new Ministry of Tourism. There has, of course, been a recurrent problem of Brits behaving badly on the Costas, with some serious incidents and fatalities in beachside bars. The underworld of British crooks who have fled there have given the area another nickname, 'the Costa del Crime.'

Above: Palma in Majorca – the Balearic Islands still offer some of the cheapest and most accessible holidays in the sun.

The main trend though, rarely reported in the press, has been a growing confidence of holidaymakers, who increasingly want to stay half board or self catering so they can try local restaurants and eat local dishes. They want hire cars to travel inland and explore the villages away from the tourist hot spots. They now spend more time sightseeing than sunbathing. And they are more prepared than ever before to attempt to speak a little Spanish. Gone are the days when all the British holidaymakers wanted to do was to bake on the beaches and eat burger and fries in what was Blackpool-on-the-Med. This was in any case, a parody of what was happening in just a few of the big resorts. Now there are many more, like Jo Crofts, a retired bus driver from Preston, who sees his annual holiday on the Costas as an opportunity to become more fluent in Spanish. 'I used to be a roast beef and yorkshire man over there, didn't eat their food, didn't speak to them apart from in English. Then one day we went to a village and I started to try to speak to the people about their lives and of course I couldn't. Well, that spurred me on. I went to classes to learn Spanish. Now I can more than hold me own talking to them. I can go anywhere and understand what they're saying, it's much better now, it's wonderful.'

THE HIPPY TRAIL

It was 1967 and the summer of love. Long hair and eastern-style kaftans were everywhere, the emblems of rebellion. Psychedelic music, flower power, the pill, LSD and the hippie counterculture seemed to offer an alternative way of life to disenchanted British youth. This was the era of the generation gap and the war with the 'straight' world of the married and the mortgaged had never been more fierce.

The so-called youth revolution had a far-reaching impact on many aspects of British life but one of its least documented effects was to introduce a new concept of alternative holidays and independent travel. No self-respecting, single young person would now want to go away on holiday with their parents, as had been the case in the past. The new trend was to go away with friends, preferably abroad. In the early 60s even Cliff Richard had seemed a little subversive in the hit movie *Summer Holiday*, when he abandoned traditional family holidays and took the 'Young Ones' off touring Europe on board a converted London double-decker bus. Just a few years later many were condemning Cliff as tame, conformist and old-fashioned.

The young people of the counterculture were not only looking for more adventure, but also for an experience that would transform their lives. Some made for the Greek Islands and Morocco, where they found a more exotic culture and a more relaxed attitude to soft drugs. The most adventurous of all headed for India on the Hippy Trail, one of the most vivid expressions of the new youth rebellion. For many young people, the journey to India was part of a broader experimentation with free love and drugs, the ultimate goal being spiritual enlightenment in a mysterious, pre-industrial world, untainted by western society. They were widely condemned as a public nuisance, an embarrassment to the British nation and a danger to themselves – and for a few the dream did indeed turn sour. Nevertheless, what they were doing was in its own way ground-breaking and hugely influential on future developments in the holiday industry. They brought back stories of exciting new destinations which filtered into the popular consciousness of the 70s, initiating the post-war trend of independent travel. The hippies pioneered backpacking and were among the first travellers to go to the Spanish resorts of Torremolinos, Ibiza and Benidorm. Ironically, they unwittingly broadened the map of the package holiday industry with their discovery of the exotic wonders of faraway places like Morocco, Turkey and Goa.

The Hippy Trail was well-trodden in the 1960s and 70s, but the origins go back much earlier than flower power. There were pioneer hippies in the first half of

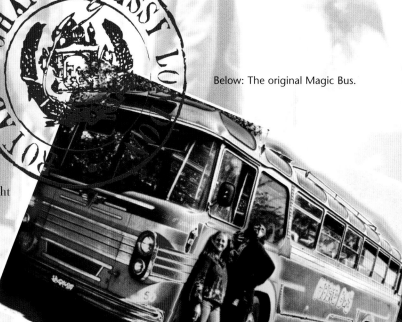

Below: The original Magic Bus.

Left: Tim Hunt (second from left) aboard the Magic Bus in 1972.

Below: Guru Sai Baba, believed by his followers to be a living god.

the century beating a path to the East in search of mysticism and enlightenment. The Himalayas were a major draw, home to the mythical Shangri-La, where by legend a utopian community lived in the remote mountain valleys. An Indian guru, Krishnamurti, was brought to Britain in the 1920s by the Theosophical Society who believed in the existence of spiritual masters, superior evolved beings who lived for thousands of years high up in the Himalayas. The Masters descended from the mountains from time to time in the form of a new World Teacher who would bring wisdom to the masses. Krishnamurti was proclaimed as the living incarnation of a Master and caused quite a stir when he arrived in Britain, with thousands coming to hear him speak. He was the first of the

131

THE HIPPY TRAIL

Indian gurus to make an impact and would inspire later generations to seek out gurus of their own.

In the 1960s Britain was flirting with Indian culture. The Beatles had adopted the Maharishi Mahesh Yogi, who brought transcendental meditation (T.M.) to the West and invited the Beatles, Mia Farrow and other celebrities to visit his ashram at Rishikesh. Saffron-robed young people were chanting Hare Krishna on the streets of London, gurus from India were speaking at public meetings, curry houses were appearing on the high street and writers were bringing Eastern mysticism into Western consciousness. Gavin Kilty, from Harwich, had dropped out from his job as a factory office clerk and arrived in London in the 60s to live in a hippy commune on Eel Pie island on the River Thames. 'I remember walking around Kensington, Notting Hill and Portobello Road and you'd see Indian paraphernalia all over the place. Travellers would come back from India, we'd all sit around in the commune and listen to them, thinking they were full of wisdom and allure, talking about this wonderful, magical place.'

This was a different type of tourism, a spiritual tourism, where the protagonists were 'travellers' rather than mere tourists and it was more than just a holiday, it was about self discovery. They gave up jobs, rejected western values and dropped out.

Top: Hippies chilling out with music in the sunshine. Clothing was optional.

Above: Eve Green left her home in Bradford in 1976 to follow the Hippie Trail.

Many hippies set off east with vague plans to follow the overland trail to Australia but with no firm ideas about how they were going to get there, how they were going to support themselves or how long they were going to be away. Spontaneity was the key. For Gavin Kilty, 'You didn't plan, man, you just went with the flow. India was the Mecca of street cred, everything we aspired to, the tales, the mystery, the magic.' He felt a natural drawing to India. 'I don't know how it happened but I was just standing in the middle of a busy road one day, a friend of mine asked me if I fancied going to India, I threw the i-ching and decided to go on the spot.'

Tim Hunt had just left Leeds University where he'd been studying economics and wanted a taste of something other than the business world. 'I thought vaguely about going to Australia, that's where I set off for, but India was the shopping centre for spiritual pursuits so I thought I'd stop there. I never did make it to Australia.'

Eve Green was already established in her career, she had a good job at Bradford University, owned a car and a home. 'But I was bored, I needed an adventure. I was dissatisfied with life in England and longed for something different.'

Going to the travel agent and planning the itinerary was not the normal way to do the overland trail. Nevertheless, there was a well defined route, passed on through word of mouth by travellers who had already made the journey. The overland route taken by most hippies was to head across Europe to Greece, then on to Istanbul in

Below: The guru Krishnamurti, brought to Britain in the 1920s by the Theosophical Society.

Bottom: Another incarnation of the Magic Bus.

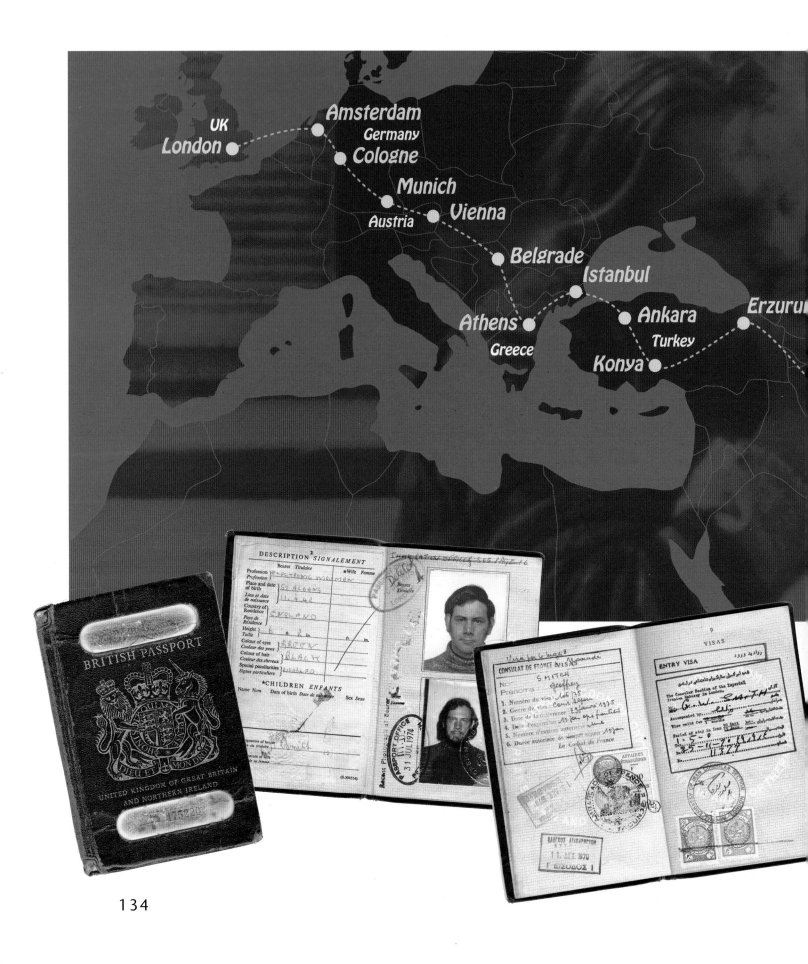

Above: The long and winding Hippie Trail.

Opposite: Geoffrey Smith's much-travelled passport.

Left: Travellers sought enlightenment from holy men such as this one in Maharashtra, India.

Turkey where they crossed into Asia. After this they continued by a number of routes to Iran, then through to Tehran and on to Afghanistan. They continued following the well-beaten track through Herat, Kandahar and Kabul. From Kabul they crossed the Khyber Pass into Pakistan, followed the Grand Trunk Road through Peshawar to Lahore and then finally arrived in India near Amritsar in the Punjab.

It was common to set off with little or no money, and to trust that you'd make it to the place you were destined to be. Hitch-hiking was popular but the most memorable form of transport was the Magic Bus – colourful, ramshackle buses that ran between London, Amsterdam, Athens and Asia. Nicknamed the 'tragic bus' it was cheap, very basic and liable to breakdown as the passengers embarked on the epic

THE HIPPY TRAIL

journey east. It wasn't run in a particularly commercial way, the organisation was casual and if you were a mechanic or hot with a spanner, you'd pay only for petrol. One traveller recalls, 'You got on the bus with your three days' worth of sandwiches and water, a sleeping bag and hoped for the best. If the bus stopped a few times a day for a trip to the toilet you were lucky. The worst part was not being able to drink for fear of when the next toilet stop might be. Most of the time, it travelled and travelled and travelled. London to Athens took around three full days.'

The original Magic Bus was a battered old coach bought by Brit Greg Williams in Delhi while he was bumming around India in 1970. It had had a number of uses from transporting books around Oxford University to carrying sheep and chickens around Asia. Greg advertised a trip to Kabul, Afghanistan at $10 a head and surprisingly enough thirty passengers booked in the space of a few hours. The seats were rock hard and the engine deafening, but two days later they arrived safely in Kabul, black with dirt and exhausted but having had a good time. Soon after, the bus was decorated, fitted with gold lamé seats and brightly coloured lights inside, and

Above: Sights such as these greeted travellers when they reached Kathmandu.

136

paintings on the outside. Big banners were added to each side saying Europe and Asia. The bus was a sight to behold as it plied its way through the desert at night, all lights blazing and winking at other vehicles on the road. From this small start other hippies bought old boneshakers and began operating a very irregular service every few days or weeks along the trail as Magic Buses. There were no timetables but everyone knew that the Magic Bus left from the American Express building in Amsterdam. People would turn up and when there were enough passengers one would leave. As it went east, passengers would get on and off and by the time it reached Asia the cargo would include babies, chickens, goats, sacks of rice, veiled women and beggars with a few riding on the roof.

As the number of Brits wanting to travel east on the Magic Buses increased, services were extended to London. Tim Hunt got on board at Victoria Station in London in 1972. 'I sat on the bus for over a week to get to Afghanistan. I took enough food to get past Austria, no-one could even afford to buy a coffee there. The atmosphere was great. There was lots of hash-smoking, people playing guitars, home made instruments, singing, we looked like Jesus freaks.'

Above: Baghwan Rajneesh addresses devotees at his ashram in the 70s

Gavin Kilty hitched to Istanbul before picking up the Magic Bus. 'Everyone knew that that the Magic Bus left from the Pudding Shop, that's where people met. You turned up and there was a noticeboard telling you when the next Magic Bus would go. We were all of the same ilk, the driver was a freak like the rest of us. There was lots of good music, it was great fun on board. Outside was different. Iran was a frightening, awful place, we just put our heads down and got through as fast as possible.'

Geoffrey Smith had just been sacked from his job – he was an apprentice plumber in 1962 and the practice at the time was to get rid of apprentices as soon as they qualified and take on a new cheaper recruit. 'I didn't know what to do, so on a whim I thought I might go off and see all the places I'd heard about in school. I didn't have much money so I went on foot.' Geoffrey walked to India. It took him seven months to get there. He had been living in Welwyn Garden City in Hertfordshire at the time and started the walk from the ferry port in France. 'I started off with 115 pounds on my back with everything from walking boots to water bottle and compass. By Athens I'd abandoned virtually everything including my razor and had just one spare pair of clothes.' Geoffrey did 20-25 miles a day and survived on very little money, sleeping rough for most of the trip. 'Petrol stations were a good place to crash and I even slept in a graveyard. I ended up being arrested for vagrancy in both Hamburg and Syria.' Money was tight and by the time he got to the YMCA in Lahore he had everything stolen. 'To make ends meet on the way I sold my blood in the Middle East where you could make £100 for a pint. I taught English in Beirut, I fixed cars and I did some plumbing work. Eventually I wore my shoes out so I made some using an old tyre.' He fell ill several times and ended up in hospital in Afghanistan with hepatitis. By the time he made it to Pakistan his money

Below: What they learned in the east, hippie travellers were keen to share on their return.

THE HIPPY TRAIL

had run out. There he bumped into a couple who were on their way to Australia overland on a Greenline bus. They had started out from Stevenage in Herts, just five miles from where Geoffrey lived. They came to his rescue and took him all of the rest of the way to Bombay. 'I'm so glad I did it. It really broadened my outlook. If I hadn't done it, I probably would have been weighed down with a mortgage, half a dozen kids and a job I hated.'

One of the big attractions of the road to the East was the many opportunities it provided to buy cheap dope and smoke it with little chance of detection or prosecution. The Hippy Trail passed through countries where cannabis was cultivated and where there was little or no attempt to prevent its use. In some Himalayan countries like Nepal, cannabis was actually legal. The path trodden by the hippies quickly became a thoroughfare for drug use, drug dealing and and drug smuggling. 'It was fantastic for us, we were harassed by the police all the time in England, but in these countries there was a different attitude, they saw smoking a joint as normal. They accepted it, you weren't worried about being arrested' says Dave Sherman, a student at the University of East Anglia in 1971. 'I can't really remember getting to India I was so spaced out practically all the way there.' Stories of the wasted lives of middle class students who idealistically journeyed east, only to become hopeless addicts or to be arrested and imprisoned, regularly appeared in the popular press – and were often grossly

Above: Gavin Kilty hitch-hiked through northern India into the Himalayas to study under the Dalai Lama in Dharamsala.

Opposite top: American hippies living in caves in Crete in the 1960s.

Opposite bottom: The Hippie Trail passed through countries where cannabis was cultivated and readily available.

exaggerated. Yet, despite this sensationalism, the dangers were real enough to make some travellers turn their back on drugs altogether. Tim Hunt got to Afghanistan via a mixture of buses, hitching, camper vans and walking. 'I had this really cosmic experience there, lying down looking up at the stars in the Afghan sky, smoking some Afghani black, really strong stuff. But I ended up unable to move, thinking I was never going to come out of it alive. I met all these Westerners in travellers' haunts who were returning from India. Some of them looked really rough. They were ill, hepatitis and so on. They had horror stories to tell of how they'd been ripped off and how sick they'd been. I decided then and there that if I was going to survive in India then I had to be a veggie and stay off drugs.'

There were, of course, no tourist guidebooks at the time to direct the hippies travelling into unknown territory but few of them felt the need for one. According to Jacquie Kilty, who hit the trail in 1973, 'You learnt things through word of mouth. You heard about cheap hotels to stay in, you were always talking to people, hearing about their adventures, swapping tales. There was always someone around to answer questions. There was such a strong sense of communication, of storytelling. Word of mouth was our guide and we used our own initiative.' Nevertheless, there were spiritual guidebooks that were read on the trail. One that virtually everyone came across was *Be Here Now* by Ram Dass, full of wise sayings like *Here We Are Here & Now, That's All There Is And If It Isn't Beautiful, Man, There's Nothing* and *Buddha's 4 Noble Truths*. There was also 'a cookbook for a sacred life' offering advice on diet, meditation and yoga.

In fact, one of the most famous series of modern day guidebooks was born out of the Hippie Trail. In 1973 Tony Wheeler, a graduate from the London Business School took off to travel overland through Asia to Australia with his wife Maureen before returning to start a 'standard business school job.' After hitch-hiking to Sydney and arriving with just 27 cents left between them, they found themselves besieged with questions about how they did it. They sat down and wrote a kitchen table account of their travels which they stapled together and sold through local booksellers. The result, *Across Asia on the Cheap*, was a big hit and the first of the Lonely Planet books. The series made its mark with guidebooks that went off the beaten track with an adventurous approach to travel assuming, as one reviewer put it, 'that you knew how to get your

THE HIPPY TRAIL

luggage off the carousel' and asked travellers themselves to contribute ideas of hotels and restaurants in a democratic way. Ten years later, western travellers in South East Asia were more often than not clutching their own well-thumbed copy of a Lonely Planet guide and Bill Gates, chairman of Microsoft, tried to buy the business.

Our interviews suggest that there were broadly three types of traveller on the Hippy Trail: the tourist, the hedonist and the spiritual seeker. The tourist was on an adventure, travelling to the main tourist sites; the hedonist was in search of a good time, free love and easy drugs; and the seeker was looking for answers to the big

questions in life from the many gurus of India. A lot of the travellers, of course, combined elements of all three and others went through different stages on their journey, beginning as sightseers or drug users and ending as seekers. Gavin Kilty, who headed for India in 1970, found that mind-altering drug experiences led him to discover a spiritual path, 'LSD and other psychedelics took you away from the real world and into the spirit world. There's always been a tradition of using psychedelics to have mystical experiences. It was so revealing you'd think, "I never knew these things." You couldn't do drugs all the time, there had to be a way of getting this without drugs. And then you heard about people who had got it through meditation.'

Gavin arrived in India with 30 dollars to his name and after six months' wandering,

Above: The Beatles adopted the Maharishi Mahesh Yogi and introduced him to the likes of Jane Asher, Mia Farrow and Donovan.

suffering from dysentery and virtually begging on the streets, he heard about an ashram, Bodh Gaya in Bihar state, where there was free food available. Bodh Gaya was a major place of pilgrimage for Buddhists from all over the world. It was the site where the Buddha is said to have attained enlightenment while meditating under a Bodhi tree. Hungry, Gavin headed for it and here he first came into contact with Buddhist practices. Although he went for the food, he became interested in meditation and found out about the Tibetan presence in Dharamsala in the Himalayas where the exiled Dalai Lama and the Tibetan government were based. 'Something clicked. I thought, "I have to go there." So I hitched through Northern India to go and study with the Dalai Lama.' He immersed himself in Tibetan Buddhism and settled into the Western community there living in a hut. 'I forgot about the rest of the world. I had absolutely nothing. The Tibetans took me in, looked after me for years. I spent my days studying and meditating. It straightened out a lot of the confusion that came with the 60s, the current of sweet naiveté. It gave me a direction.'

Below: Although hippies arrived in India with little or no money, they soon found ways to get by and many stayed for several years.

Gavin ended up staying in Dharamsala for 14 years, during which time he met and married Jacquie, a fellow seeker, who'd left Cambridge where she was working in a wholefood cafe called Arjuna before embarking on the Hippie Trail in 1973. They survived on very little, but made cakes to sell to fellow Western pilgrims who were missing their sweet tooth. Ginger cake was the favourite. They had two children whom Gavin delivered himself half way up a mountain having taken lessons in midwifery from a Tibetan doctor.

Eve Green also lived for a time in a Buddhist community on her Indian trip. She had left her home in Bradford in 1976 and set off on a Magic Bus for India hoping to make it to Australia. *En route* she heard about an ashram, a Buddhist meditation centre at Igatpuri near Bombay and decided to try a retreat there. 'It was a very strict regime, we had to get up at 4 a.m. and we meditated. The first retreat you did you were in a hall with everyone else and from then on you were in a solitary cell which was dark, no noise, sensory deprivation, and you just meditated for four days. We were segregated into two separate parts of the compound, males and females and we didn't eat after midday, so at 5 p.m. we had lemon water and then nothing till the next day. We had a lecture in the evening and the rest of the time you were in your cell, meditating. It just blew me away. After ten days I came out and I'd had every experience from being totally blissed out to being in a state of complete shock, horror. I experienced a lot of pain then suddenly you would let go and be free from the negative sensations and you'd be at peace and feel very calm and relaxed. I had

Below and left: Hippies heading for the River Ganges and spiritual cleansing.

Opposite: Washing facilities in religious retreats were often primitive and communal.

amazing experiences, out-of-body sensations. I experienced seeing the world like a pointless painting. My whole world turned upside down.' Eve relished the austerity so much she remained in Indian ashrams for three years before returning home to England.

Many of the seekers went in search of a guru – a wise man – to guide them towards the meaning of life in a way that conventional western Christianity had failed to do. One of the most colourful gurus was Sai Baba whose ashram 'Prasanthi Nilayam' – the abode of supreme peace – was high in the hills to the north of Bangalore. Sai Baba was and still is believed by devotees to be an 'avatar, a living god.' This particular avatar looked like a version of Jimi Hendrix with his bouffant Afro hairdo. His ashram, which was built in 1950, today attracts tens of thousands on pilgrimages from all over the world, but in the early 70s word had only started to spread about his supposedly miraculous powers. There were tales of honey pouring out of pictures of goddesses, milk being expressed from eyes and Sai Baba secreting vibhuti 'sacred ash' from his hands.

Shirley Harris from London was one such seeker who came to India, in search of herself and found a new identity at Sai Baba's ashram. 'I had heard the stories of miracles and so on and wanted to see for myself. Originally I went in search of another guru but he had just died and I was told that Sai Baba was the living god. Initially people were a bit suspicious of me because there weren't many westerners then and frankly I wasn't that impressed. It wasn't much fun at the ashram. Up at 4 a.m. for meditation after sleeping on a hard floor and then join a queue to wait around for food and then another queue for darshan, one of the daily audiences with Sai Baba. I felt like leaving, but everything changed after one audience I had with the avatar. I had an overwhelming feeling of love and connectedness, I felt like I was awakening the god within and he was a means of doing it.' Shirley stayed for nine months in all and ended up living with other western pilgrims who started arriving in droves.

The ashram became somewhat of a spiritual Disneyland with pastel-coloured temples and arches and on the perimeter a panoply of mind/body/spirit souvenir shops plastered with images of Sai Baba and his teachings. It was awash with rules – 'please observe the silence and keep children under control, do not mix with the opposite sex unless closely related, do not get friendly with strangers and do not move around after "lights off" at 9 p.m.' There were rituals around food, too. Most foods were out of bounds because they provoked lust and eating in restaurants was banned too as 'you may end up sitting in the seat of someone who has had murderous thoughts.' The canteens where people did eat were sex-segregated and the diet largely boiled rice and dahl. Outside a 'thought for the day' was helpfully pinned to the tree to aid digestion.

The hippies beat a path to destinations which would later become part of the tourist trail. The Himalayas were a natural draw and a cool place to

THE HIPPY TRAIL

head for during the hot summer months in India. Early Tibetan scripts and Hindu epics told of the wondrous Himalaya where gods dwelt on high and mortals could find heaven-on-earth in hidden valleys. Nepal, the enchanting mountain kingdom, only opened up to Westerners in 1949, before when it had been the largest inhabited country yet to be explored by Europeans. The trekking business in Nepal began in 1964 when Lt Col Jimmy Roberts, an officer who served in the British Indian army, advertised his first trek in Holiday Magazine. By the time Tim Hunt arrived in the Himalayas in 1972, it was the done thing to go off on a trek in search of nirvana. He set off on his own with a map he picked up from a man in the street. After a few days he got lost just when it was starting to snow in the mountains. 'It turned into a blizzard. It got really bad and I thought I was going to die. It was freezing. I'd been walking in pumps. I was completely unprepared and then I got lost for days. I found shelter under a log thing and slept under that. On the fourth day I spotted a sherpa's village down the valley. Desperate but overjoyed, I got down there where I found these westerners sitting around in the sun having coffee. "Hey man, how you doing?" one of them said, "Which way did you come?"'

Civil servant Andy Fagg, then in his 20s, jacked in his job in London in 1982 and months later arrived in the Himalayas. 'I was entranced by the mountains, there was this pull about the Himalayas. I had this notion that I'd explore Buddhism and in Nepal I met a lot of Tibetan refugees who were so warm and open. They had something about them. I thought they were really living something. The Tibetan iconography drew me in too, it was compelling.'

Andy headed off trekking in the Mount Everest region. 'There was something about the simplicity of walking, eating, shitting and walking which was really appealing in its basic physicality. I was a mathematician and spent a lot of time in my head but to

Above: Smoking dope with a chillum in Kathmandu.

Opposite: Eve Green was captivated by the beach scene in Goa.

do something so physical was liberating. Thoughts would pass like clouds, I was in awe of the stunning beauty of the mountains as we walked. I really got in touch with myself.' With his wife, Kathy, Andy headed up to Namche Bazaar. 'We were the first group to go over a high pass since it had snowed. We got stuck in the snow. It got in everywhere, my boots froze overnight. My big mistake was putting them on in the morning. It was like wearing blocks of ice. My feet were cold, bruised and wet and my toes went completely black.' He developed frostbite in both feet and had to be carried down some of the way by a sherpa. 'We then hired two yaks to take us the three days down to Namche Bazaar. The driver was drunk and the yaks kept straying off the path. I had no idea if I was going to lose my toes. We couldn't go any further

THE HIPPY TRAIL

than Namche with the yaks because the air was too thick for them. We needed to hire a horse but didn't have a clue how to get one. Kathy went off to find someone to help. There was a familiar-looking man, a rather attractive westerner that in desperation she stopped in the hope that he would help. It turned out to be Robert Redford. He used his local contacts to get us a horse and we managed to get down to Lukla where we had a three day wait for the next flight. It took a lot of baksheesh to get us on.' Back in Kathmandu Andy slowly recovered the feeling in his feet.

The most notable area that the hippies discovered was Goa, the west coastal strip of India below Bombay with its perfect beaches and sleepy fishing villages. The hippies were the trailblazers who colonised this former Portuguese enclave, turning it into a travellers' paradise. Eve Green was delighted to find Goa's mellow 70s beach scene to which she retreated. 'The Goa thing completely blew my mind. There were these incredible parties on the beach amongst the palm trees. There'd be hundreds of candles dotted around and hundreds of people lying around playing music, stoned or kipping. The parties were really elaborate. They were like happenings, there'd be parades with people walking around on stilts. I remember someone dressed as the moon and stars who went around giving everyone a drop of acid on the tongue. I was fascinated by it all. I met some wonderful people who did yoga, something creative like painting or storytelling. There were people from around the world, a lot of Americans. I even remember women giving birth in the grass huts.'

Andy Fagg went to Goa to rest after suffering frostbite in the Himalayas. 'I just wanted to hang out on the beach and get stoned. It was all very relaxed, people would walk around naked. We lived in a shack, it was very basic with a squat toilet where a pig's snout would appear snuffling almost before you'd left your deposit! The local skunk was really strong. I remember almost hallucinating once. I was in a rickshaw and was absolutely terrified. The driver was racing, he was surely going to crash. In fact he was only doing about ten miles an hour.'

It was in Goa that Andy embarked on an experiment which was to change his life. 'When I was getting over frostbite, Kathy started stroking my feet. I thought, "This feels good." It really brought the the feeling back into my toes. We found a book on massage and on the beach, with the liberation of being without clothes, we set about working our way through the book. We tried out massage on each other and then with other travellers. I discovered I really liked it. I loved the fact that it was body-based and not brain.' Returning to Britain the following year, Andy felt that he wanted to pursue his interest in massage and not go back to being the Oxbridge mathematician that he had been. 'People went around asking me, "Did you have a nice holiday?" In fact, I'd had a life-altering experience. I didn't want to go back to the old way.' For Andy the time in India led to a change in career. He became a massage therapist and now runs a school of holistic massage.

Many others on the Hippy Trail came back and chose a different direction in their lives. Eve Green retrained as a psychotherapist, Tim Hunt came back and developed an arts and crafts business, and Gavin and Jacquie Kilty now work at a Buddhist college in Devon. Geoffrey Smith's epic trip on foot suffered a tragic turn. A week after his homecoming he was knocked down by a taxi and lost the use of his legs. But that didn't stop his adventures. He became a cabbie himself and embarked on lengthy charity trips overseas in his taxi, once going to the Iranian border. Apart from Geoffrey all these former hippies have settled in the South West of England where their presence has helped shape the New Age centres in towns like Totnes, Glastonbury and Stroud. Typically, they're self-employed, doing their own thing by setting up their own alternative businesses in arts, crafts and holistic therapies.

The hippies helped inspire various forms of spiritual tourism among the new hippies of later generations. In the Greek islands, for example, the New Age centre of Skyros has been offering all-inclusive holistic holidays for the last 20 years describing them as 'sun, sea and a sense of community.' Activities include massage, mosaic-making and mind-body retunement. The holidaymakers are called participants and live in simple huts. They help out with the running of the community by laying tables and chopping vegetables, all of which helps to create a bond. And the ashrams of India continue to attract many thousands of westerners who – following in the footsteps of the old hippies – come to recharge their spiritual batteries while living as part of a community where they eat, sleep, meditate to the guru and perform simple chores.

The main legacy of the Hippy Trail, though, was to the travel industry itself. Bohemians and hippies broke the mould of conventional holidays, bringing back stories of extraordinary places and inspiring others to follow a similar independent path. They extended the tourist map to distant lands and opened up destinations which were later popularised by backpackers and ultimately the package holiday industry. Goa is the classic example. The hippies arrived overland in the 1960s and 70s, followed by younger independent backpackers who came in on bucket shop flights in the 80s. In the early 90s Goa was appearing in brochures of new long haul package holiday destinations alongside Florida and Kenya. By the year 2000 the hippie heaven in the exotic East had become one of the popular long haul winter destinations for British tourists. India was firmly on the map of mass tourism.

Left: Hippies inspired others to follow in their tracks and many found that their experiences changed their lives forever.

HIGH SOCIETY HOLIDAYS

One of the most remarkable turnarounds in 20th century travel has been the mass marketing of holidays that once bore the exclusive hallmark of the aristocracy. Exotic safaris in the tropics or de luxe journeys on board the Orient Express once belonged to the upper classes and remained in the realm of fantasy for all but a privileged few. In the second half of the last century, however, elite holidays like these moved into the mainstream. Most popular of all among holidays once restricted to the rich are cruising and skiing. In the 1970s skiing was the fastest growing holiday industry but by the end of the century that honour had passed to cruising. And this from the ships that invented the term 'posh' – Port Out, Starboard Home gave the best views from your cabin.

Although superficially so different, cruising and skiing shared a lot in their appeal. The opportunity to experience a holiday once associated with the rich and famous was clearly an important attraction, made much of in the publicity. In an era when summer holidays abroad became available to the majority of the population, wintersun skiing holidays – usually a second holiday – maintained a certain social standing and made a subtle statement of status and wealth. Both skiing and cruising offered an escape into a dreamland of glamour and romance, with the opportunity for an active social life, proving a magnet for gold diggers and social climbers. Crucially, both types of holiday benefitted from spectacular natural phenomena – the high seas and the high peaks.

Skiing evolved out of the romantic appeal of the mountains. For centuries the Alps had been part of the aristocratic Grand Tour with well-heeled British tourists admiring the scenery, usually from a distance, *en route* across Europe. From the 1850s onwards more adventurous visitors tried their hand at mountaineering, a welcome escape for the wealthy city dweller in search of a physical challenge. In late Victorian times the higher mountains opened up to less active tourists who were discovering the delights of the Alps in summer. Winter holidays in the mountains started in 1864 following a chance conversation between a hotelier in the Swiss resort of St Moritz and a small group of British guests. Herr Badrutt boasted about the magnificent weather that could be experienced at the resort in winter and to prove his point, he offered the disbelieving guests free accomodation that winter. Not wanting to pass up the opportunity of a free holiday, the visitors willingly accepted. In fact, they stayed for five and a half months. They were so enthusiastic that back home word soon got around the upper classes and winter holidays in Switzerland quickly became the 'in' thing in high society.

The health-giving properties of mountain air were being promoted by physicians as a cure for respiratory diseases. Invalids moved from the spas, where they had

Left: Thomas Cook's 1908 Winter Sports Swiss holiday brochure.

Below: The crisp white uniforms of the ship's officers made a cruise an even more attractive prospect for some female passengers.

Opposite: As well as the elitist image, fresh air and sunshine were also common factors in skiing and cruising holidays.

traditionally gone to recuperate, to the invigorating climate of the mountains. Every mountain village in Switzerland now had the potential of turning into a year-round health and holiday resort. These early visitors, who came with the motive of restoring their health, organised their own entertainments and the more active took part in traditional winter sports like tobogganing, curling and skating. According to Robert Louis Stevenson the Alps were developing a distinctly British feel. 'In the English hotels home-played farces, tableaux vivants, and even balls enliven the evenings; Christmas and New Year are solemnized with Pantagruelian dinners and from time to time the young folks carol and revolve untunefully enough through the figures of a singing quadrille. A magazine club supplies you with everything from the *Quarterly* to the *Sunday at Home*. Grand tournaments are organised at chess, draughts, billiards and whist.' The social whirl in the mountains attracted people like the Prince of Wales, later Edward VII, who did for winter sports what the Prince Regent had done for the seaside, and the famous winter resorts of Switzerland and Austria came to share a reputation with the Riviera as cosmopolitan centres of luxury and fashion.

The British were among the biggest movers and shakers behind the development of skiing. One family was largely responsible in promoting skiing, father and son Henry and Arnold Lunn of the tour operator that later became Lunn Poly. Sir Henry Lunn organised the first winter sports package in 1898, sending British holidaymakers in the care of a ski instructor to Chamonix where they engaged in something novel, skiing downhill. Before then, skiing cross country had been the norm. To the participants it must have seemed like a working holiday because they had to climb back up the mountain everytime they skied down. By 1910 Henry Lunn had managed to persuade the mountain railway company at Murren in Switzerland, which normally only took walkers up the mountain in summer, to stay open in winter for skiers. This was the role Lunn played in popularising downhill skiing and he was also influential in the opening

Left: Tourists in the Alps, as depicted in 'Le Journal de la Jeunesse,' Paris, 1889.

of the Swiss resorts of Klosters, Murren and Wengen. 'The love of the mountains is like the love of music,' wrote his son Arnold in his *History of Skiing* (1927). 'In the mountain school, lessons of courage and endurance and initiative and good humour under adversity, lessons of imperishable value not only to the individual but to the race.'

Skiing for pleasure is essentially a 20th century phenomenon. The Ski Club of Great Britain was formed in 1903, promoting the development of British ski clubs in elite Swiss ski resorts like Davos and Wengen. At first the skiers depended on early railways, ratchet trains and buses to get them uphill, but in the 30s proper ski-lifts were built and skiing began to gain in popularity. A major expansion of ski resorts beyond Switzerland happened in the 1930s and again the British were hugely influential. One of the leading French ski resorts, Meribel, was built by a Brit. In 1938, Major Peter Lindsay and a group of former Indian army skiing friends were looking for a site in France on which to develop their favourite sport. After purchasing a few acres, Lindsay named the area Meribel after a local hamlet because it sounded better in English than Les Allues, the French name for the valley. Today Meribel still plays host to more British skiers than any other European resort.

The 1920s and 30s are often regarded as the golden age of skiing, when it was the winter pastime of the smart set, filling the gap in the social season during the dead months after Christmas. They were the only ones who could afford the time, the travel, the teachers and the expensive trappings to go skiing. Days spent on the slopes stimulated a jaded appetite and the apres-ski scene was very active. Ladies packed ball gowns for the parties, tea dances were popular and fondues were all the rage. The SCGB began organising tour parties skiing in the 30s and the buzz came home to Britain too – the first dry ski school was opened at Lillywhites in London in 1932.

It wasn't until after World War II that skiing started to change from being the most exclusive of holiday pursuits to something much more widely undertaken. This began with the influence of returning troops who had their first experience of skiing whilst in service and wanted to continue with the winter recreation. John Wyllie, who runs an art gallery in London, chose a ski trip for his first foreign holiday in 1949. 'I had heard about skiing from friends in the army, so I decided to go to Arosa in Switzerland. As I went up on the mountain railway, the rain changed to sleet and then to snow and then emerged into beautiful sunshine. It was like a miracle. I was very excited to discover that there was blackcherry jam and butter in the hotel because rationing was still on at home. I had the old wooden skis, in those days there were very few ski lifts so you'd walk up the slope with sealskins attached to the bottom of your skis for extra grip. It took about two and a half hours to climb to the top and five to ten minutes to ski down!'

Above: John Wyllie went on his first foreign holiday in 1949, skiing in Arosa, Switzerland.

HIGH SOCIETY HOLIDAYS

The demand for more adventurous holidays, especially among young people, together with a steady increase in car ownership and better access to ski resorts, all helped to promote the new trend in the 1950s. And there were rapid improvements in the equipment used, making skiing more manageable for those who couldn't see the sense in careering downhill out of control with two impossibly long wooden planks stuck on the end of their feet. Elizabeth Hussey from London first went skiing in St Anton in Austria in 1959. 'I got hooked that first season, skiing was terribly addictive. It was the challenge, the excitement and the speed together with the beautiful mountains. You couldn't help but make friends once you've fallen down five times. It was fantastic to get out into the sunshine at that cold, dark time of year. The fresh air was almost too much, I used to go to sleep for a few hours when I got in from the slopes. You could always tell those people at home who'd been skiing from the suntans in February and March. I went skiing every year after that.'

The ski boom really began in the 1960s. Wooden skis and leather boots were phased out and replaced by high performance fibreglass and composite skis and plastic boots, making skiing equipment more lightweight. The more advanced designs also made the sport safer, dramatically reducing the incidence of injury. The idea of staying in chalets took off, giving the skiing holiday more of a 'house party' atmosphere.

Above: A Victorian engraving showing an outward bound vessel passing the P&O liner 'Victoria' as she headed home through the Suez Canal.

Opposite top: Relaxing on deck on the way to India, circa 1890.

Opposite bottom: Little had changed 30 years later when these passengers sailed for India aboard the 'Rajputana.'

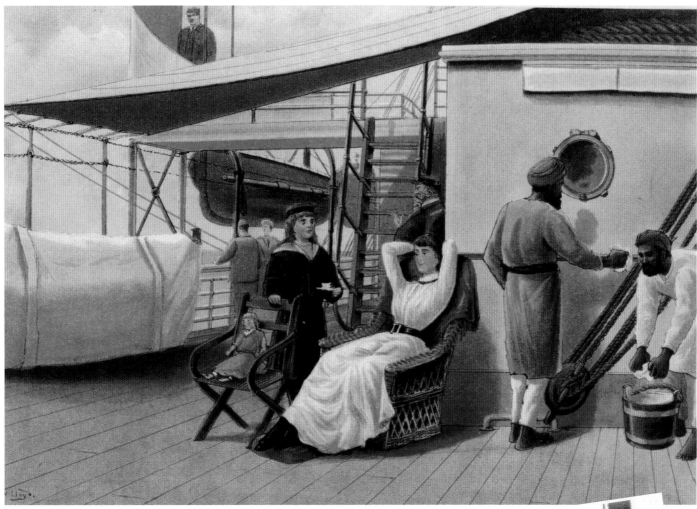

Skiers were looked after by chalet girls (or boys), generally skiing enthusiasts, who cooked and cleaned in return for meagre wages and the chance to indulge in their favourite pastime when off duty. The charter jets flew in British tourists in their thousands, particularly the young and single who wanted to try out the sport of the rich. The elite skiers continued to visit Switzerland or Austria but the newer winter sports fans headed for the purpose-built resorts in France which still attract the bulk of British skiers.

Such was the popularity of skiing that by the late 60s over half of those going on skiing package holidays had never

HIGH SOCIETY HOLIDAYS

skied before. School skiing trips were hugely influential in the 1960s and 70s, introducing a new generation to the sport while they were still at that totally fearless, indestructable stage in their lives. By the end of the 1970s there were an estimated half a million skiers in Britain.

Whilst skiing drew on its upper class pedigree for much of its original appeal, cruising enjoyed an even more illustrious tradition of exclusive luxury reminiscent of a bygone age. Before the era of the jet aircraft, those travelling overseas did so on luxurious ocean liners. Legendary names like the *Mauretania*, the *Queen Mary*, the *Queen Elizabeth*, the *Ile-de-France*, the *Normandie* and not forgetting the ill-fated *Titanic*, ploughed their way across the Atlantic offering a lavish lifestyle where one

could eat well, drink well, socialise and form significant relationships with other well-heeled companions. The ships were deeply class-ridden. Passengers were divided into three classes, with the social elite in the first class cabins enjoying the high life, the less affluent in the less desirable second class cabins and the emigrants looking to start a new life in the New World housed below deck in basic conditions. Even though it was the rich and famous passengers who attracted all the attention, with society columns detailing the travel plans of celebrities and the luxury of life on board, the major shipping lines actually earned most of their money from emigrants. When that lucrative trade started to dry up in the early part of the 20th century, the shipping lines

Above: The 'Queen Mary,' one of an elite fleet of liners offering luxurious trans-Atlantic travel.

had to find another source of income. The answer was cruising.

Scheduled cruises to remote and exotic places had been introduced by shipping lines as an off-season revenue earner for their liners. Even the largest ships such as Cunard's *Mauretania* sought to spend the winters away from the ferocious North Atlantic by taking groups of millionaires around the Riviera. A life on the ocean waves always had a romantic appeal and passengers were invited to enjoy the sunshine, the sea, the social life, the comfort and the luxury of cruising between interesting ports of call. The salt air environment was considered

therapeutic by many physicians and 'take a long sea voyage' was often the advice given to patients. The Hamburg-Amerika line in Germany built the world's first dedicated cruise ship in 1900. The *Prinzessin Victoria Luise* was only 400 foot long and designed to resemble the royal yachts of Europe, thus attracting an exclusive clientele. Each cabin had its own bedroom, sitting room and bathroom. By the late 1920s, world cruising had become an established social ritual for the wealthy. The *Franconia*, for example, would take guests to Bali, Macassar, Bangkok and Saigon. In Britain, cruises to the Mediterranean were popular while Americans headed for the Caribbean. Without a doubt, cruising was a hit amongst the leisured rich who could

Top: As with skiing, school cruise trips offered youngsters a whole new experience. This is one such group aboard the 'Uganda' in 1978.

Above: When the Orient Express train's route became no longer viable, it linked with the Orient Express cruise liner to take passengers from Venice to Istanbul.

afford to take life easy. One lady, Miss Clara MacBeth, was said to have spent 14 years cruising.

During World War II ocean liners became troop ships and before returning to peacetime duties they were used to repatriate prisoners, settle refugees in new countries or even transport Britain's GI brides to America. Transatlantic passenger traffic continued to build steadily after the war reaching its peak in 1957, although its death knell came the following year when Pan American offered the first non-stop transatlantic crossing in a Boeing 707. Immediately, the jets captured half the traffic and noticeably few ships were built after that date. Those that were, like the *QE2* in 1967, were built with cruising in mind.

In the 1960s, the most popular cruise ship in Britain was the Royal Mail Lines' *Andes* which was converted for cruising in 1959. Two and three-week sailings were often booked a year or more in advance. According to purser John Draffin, 'She was much like a floating country club, the "Who's Who" of Britain would be on board. Passengers in the best suites brought along their own servants. While we always carried a full dance band, the demand was, in fact, for very limited entertainment. It was a very quiet, elegant lifestyle on board. The *Andes* catered to aristocratic Britain.'

Cruising was a status symbol which, from the 1960s onwards, was becoming affordable beyond the smart set. Middle-class families were the first to get on board. The formality of life on board, with the dressing for dinner and the tipping of uniformed staff, was all part of the appeal. Aspiring to a better way of life, some took a cruise holiday as a statement of having arrived at a certain level in society. Linda Corby recalls going on a cruise to the Caribbean with her parents in the late 60s, 'We felt we were terribly posh; it really was the jetset thing to do.' By the next decade, passengers on luxury liners included a few men and women from the most humble of backgrounds. One of them was Fred Baker, a lorry driver from London's East End. He had just retired, lost his wife and cashed in an insurance policy, blowing it on the cruise. 'I couldn't believe I was there on the *QE2*, living the life of Riley on a luxury cruise. I felt so proud. I had my dinner jacket and bow tie on in the evenings and I was mixing with the best of them. I kept it a secret from the family but when I came back and told them what I'd done and showed them the photos, they were amazed. People like us didn't go on cruises in those days, it was something very special.' The pinnacle of social success was to be invited to dine at the captain's table. Etiquette was maintained for dinner, with course after course of the most elaborate food being served.

Audrey Witta, who worked as a sales assistant in Harrods, treated herself to a cruise and ended up dining at the top table. 'Why shouldn't I be at the captain's table? I thought I was as good as they were and I was going to prove it.'

As well as the converted liners and purpose-built cruise ships, another option was to cruise on a banana boat, a freighter that would take a few passengers as well as its normal cargo (often fruit). Some were luxurious affairs, but others offered cruises on

HIGH SOCIETY HOLIDAYS

the cheap where the crew weren't always as welcoming as the uniformed staff on the oceangoing liners. The unofficial slogan was 'every banana a guest, every passenger a pest.' On the cheaper cruises the cabins could be primitive. Blackpool landlady Pat Mancini sometimes took the banana boat from Liverpool to Las Palmas on her winter holidays in the 1970s. 'I used to say to everyone I was going on a cruise to the Canaries. Oh you felt like you were really something. People thought you were really rich but, of course, you didn't say it was on a banana boat. Well, the cabin we used to have, you couldn't get lower in the ship and all you could hear was the ship's pistons juddering and it was so small, just two bunks and a corner sink. You dressed up all the same for dinner and I had this long gold evening gown. I thought I was the bee's knees.'

As well as a statement of wealth, the appeal of cruising to the post-war holidaymaker lay in its ease. 'Once you'd unpacked, that was it, you didn't have to move for the rest of the trip, you could just relax with a book,' recalls Lydia Howe from Hertfordshire, who cruised around the Mediterranean in the 1960s. 'And the ship spirited you effortlessly from port to port, it couldn't have been easier.' For a lot of cautious holidaymakers embarking on their first trip abroad, a cruise was ideal for the safety net it offered. You could spend the day in fascinating but

Above and opposite: Barbara Holman became a big fan of cruising after her first romantic encounter aboard the 'Calypso' in Scandinavia (far right).

risky countries like Morocco, then retreat back to the haven of the ship in the evening where the food, water and hygiene could be trusted. For this reason, cruises have always been popular with the elderly and more recently families who are safe in the knowledge that their children will not get lost and will be catered for on board.

There was also a tremendous romance associated with cruising. In the early years of the transatlantic liners, social climbers would aim to book a deckchair or a place at the dining table next to eligible partners and ambitious parents hoped to get their offspring matched by the end of the trip. Honeymooners took to the high seas and in 1977 the television series *The Love Boat* was broadcast worldwide, reinforcing a romantic image of cruising. Uniformed crew were often the object of romantic fantasy and with passengers thrown together for days on end, cruises developed a reputation

for being a hotbed of sexual activity. Fun-loving singles, divorcees and widows came on board looking for a mate. They were encouraged to join in with all of the activities on board in the same manner as a holiday camp and consequently often met potential partners. Barbara Holman, a divorcee from Stockport, had no thoughts of love when she took her young daughter on a cruise to Norway in the late 70s. 'It was on the SS *Calypso*. I didn't know a soul on board but I was looking out for some people when I noticed a man on a settee reading a book. The next day he came up and chatted to me and we played board games with my daughter. He asked me to go to the cinema, it was one of those funny Pink Panther films, and he took hold of my hand in the dark. The next evening we went to the disco, dancing to Rod Stewart *Do Ya Think I'm Sexy* and from then on we were inseparable. I don't know if it was the daiquiri cocktails or the midnight sun but we ended up spending a lot of time in the cabin, it was a very active fortnight!'

By the 1990s, cruising had seduced the British public. In spite of its small, elitest origins, it became the biggest growing holiday sector in the country and Britain is now the second-largest cruise market in the world after the USA. The rapid increase started in the late 80s when the tour operators began offering all-inclusive cruises at package holiday prices and in 1995 P&O launched the *Oriana*, the first cruise ship purpose-built for the UK market. In the mid-1990s the major tour operators smelled success when the number of British holidaymakers going on cruises increased by an average of over 20% each year making it the great success of the British holiday industry at the end of the century. What were once the holiday pleasures of high society could now be enjoyed by the masses.

BACKPACKING AND BEACH PARTIES

CAPE TRIBULATION
KURANDA
TABLELANDS
OUTBACK

For Affordable Fun, Action and Adventure

In the last quarter of the 20th century one of the biggest changes in holidaymaking has been the growth of independent youth travel. A new creature was born, the backpacker, recognisable from its rucksack, money belt, sandals and colourful, ethnic clothes. Britain's youth seized upon travel and made it not only one of their main leisure activities but a rite of passage from youth to adulthood. Nowadays, for many young people, roughing it on a round-the-world ticket signals the passage to maturity. The hippies may have been the early pioneers of independent youth travel but it was the backpackers of the late 70s and 80s who turned it into a trend.

Whereas for the flower children travelling was an act of rebellion, dropping out and being different, two decades later independent youth travel had become an act of conformity, one of the things you did after leaving school or college or before settling down to a partner, mortgage and children. By the late 1990s, one in five students were taking a gap year between their A levels and their degree course with the intention of travelling. At the same time there was the emergence of another related trend among Britain's holidaying youth, that of a new hedonism. Young holidaymakers wanted sun, sea, sangria, stimulants and sex. Club 18-30 holidays were reputed to supply condoms along with the tickets and resorts like Ibiza developed a drug-fuelled clubbing culture.

For many young people in the 1960s, 70s and 80s the first taste of independent youth travel was thumbing a lift. Hitch-hiking was at its height during this period, a way for young people to get around at no cost. Something akin to hitching had been practised for centuries, but it really came into its own with the development of motor transport. Many thousands thumbed lifts on the Home Front in the last war, when it was endorsed by the government as a way of saving fuel costs. Beatniks and flower children short of cash were the post-war pioneers of hitch-hiking for pleasure in the summer months . In the 70s this became much more widespread, with a big increase in the numbers of young people hitching. Many of them were now heading out of Britain. One fashion was to spend a few weeks in summer in the warmer and cheaper countries of the Mediterranean.

This page: Australia has become a major destination for yong backpackers with gap-year students benefiting from year-long visas which allow them to take a job down under.

Opposite: The trail the hippies blazed to the East has never been allowed to go cold.

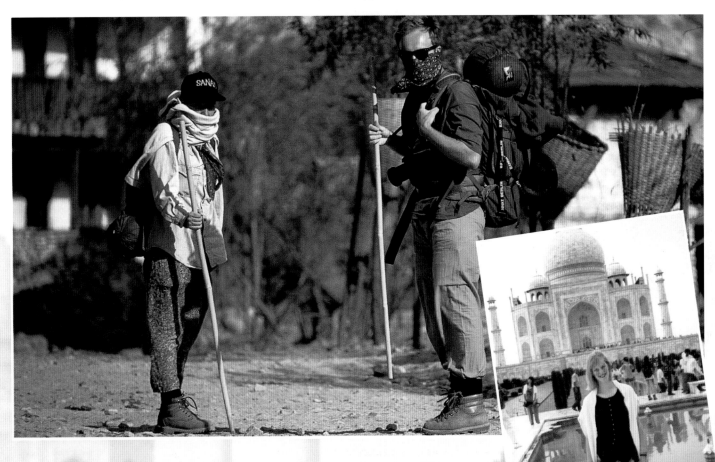

In the mid-70s designer Ginette Ruthven used to hitch across Europe from her home in North Wales to the Greek islands. 'I could get to Greece in under three days. I thought hitching was a fantastic way to get to know the countries you were travelling through, by talking to the people who gave you lifts. As you got into the car, you were stepping straight into their lives. So many times I've been taken by families back to their home to meet all the relatives, be fed and have a bed for the night in everything from a palazzo to a hermit's hovel. Hitching was so popular at the time that there would be queues of up to 20 people waiting at the well-known pick-up points like Orly, south of Paris.

'I would sometimes hold a bunch of flowers in an attempt to get a lift. Dutch lorry drivers were great, they seemed to go really long distances. Hitching was definitely a two-way thing, they might give you a lift, but you were expected to talk non-stop and entertain the driver so that he didn't fall asleep. They'd get quite stroppy if you stopped chatting. Hitching was positively encouraged in some of the Communist countries. I remember in Poland not many people had cars and the drivers made you sign a chit when they picked you up. Apparently they were given petrol coupons as a reward for picking up hikers!

'The route went down through Yugoslavia to Greece. I remember once in Macedonia I was in a lorry that was travelling illegally at night with no lights on. We were stopped by police, so the driver decided to continue to the Greek border across fields of cut corn. The view as the sun came up across the corn was amazing. Once I got to Greece I'd spend weeks island hopping. Ios seemed to be the place where all the young people

BACKPACKING AND BEACHPARTIES

went, Mykonos was the other. You could live all
summer for very little, hanging out on the
beaches, chatting, philosophising and reading
books; it was all very mellow. I slept on the
beach like a lot of other people. It felt very
natural and basic and the feeling was, "Why
sleep in a bed when you do that the rest of
the year?"'

   Hitching as a way of going abroad
became less popular in the late 1970s and
80s as others means of transport became
affordable for young people. There was an
upsurge in the numbers who travelled
across the Channel with their motorbikes
and rode them through Europe. While in
the 60s the Mods and Rockers had been
content to drive down to the southeast coast of England
for their so-called 'battles on the beaches,' the young motorcycle devotees and
gangs were now looking for something more adventurous. Inspired by films like *Easy
Rider*, riding down to the Mediterranean coast and to Greece became a cult
summer holiday experience. Others in their teens and early 20s did it in
cars, but the prevalence of cars didn't always lead to more lifts for those
hitching. Former hitch-hiker Simon Sykes from Portsmouth believes that the
old communality of the road was killed off by the new generation of young
Thatcherite car owners. 'The attitude changed to, "It's my car, I don't see
why I should share it." Before then it had been more a case of, "You're lucky
enough to have a car, you owe me a lift."'

   For a lot of young people in the late 1970s and 80s, their first experience of
backpacking was with the Inter-Rail scheme in Europe which brought
continental rail travel to within the reach of many students and graduates.
Inter-Railing started in 1972 and was an initiative of the International Union of
Railways designed to encourage rail travel among young people, a previously
neglected sector of the travel market. The ticket cost just £33 to the under-26s
and offered unlimited rail travel across Europe for a month. Adventurous young
people had the Continent at their feet, complete with the rigours of the Iron
Curtain. The original group of 19 countries who joined the scheme were: Austria,
Belgium, Denmark, Ireland, Great Britain, Finland, France, both East and West
Germany, Hungary, Italy, Luxembourg, the Netherlands, Norway, Portugal, Spain,
Sweden, Switzerland and Yugoslavia. Tony Fielding from Shropshire, a railway
enthusiast, loved the idea of a student version of the Orient Express. He first went
Inter-Railing in the summer of 1983. 'I wanted to see Europe but didn't have much
money and Inter-Railing seemed like a much safer way of doing it than hitching.
That little brown book was your passport, all you had to do was write down your
destination and away you went. The Thomas Cook Continental Timetable was the
most valuable possession after the rail pass and part of the interest was working out
how to get from one place to the next. You could get on and off as often as you

wanted and by sleeping on the train you saved on accommodation. I remember once wanting to get down to Barcelona but I'd missed the train from Paris, so I chose a nice long night journey to Lucerne in Switzerland instead so that I could get a good sleep. In the morning I went back up to Paris to catch the connection down to Spain. You could do things like that! I'm sure it was pretty strange for all those pristine commuters going into work in the morning to have a slightly grubby Inter-Rail traveller sitting next to them.'

The Inter-Rail scheme was an instant success. Over 70,000 passes were sold Europe-wide in its first few months and over the years more countries joined in including those on the fringes of Europe like Morocco and more of the Communist Bloc. Not only did it bring the youth of Europe together, it also created an uneasy alliance of warring countries. Jerry Green, a student from Reading University, experienced this firsthand in 1985 on a trip from Greece to Turkey. 'The journey into Istanbul from Greece was like a microcosm of Greco-Turkish relations. The six-carriage train arriving from Athens was halved at Alexandroupolis when we boarded so it was very cramped. Greek railways already represented the nadir of European rail comfort at the time but to our disbelief, the crowded three-carriage train was reduced to two at the border post. And then the train just sat there for over four hours in the soaring heat for no apparent reason. Maybe it was reluctant to go the few yards over into Turkey. Our passports were taken away for inspection along with those of other passengers. It was only when someone suggested going for a drink at a nearby cafe to save us from dehydration that we found all the passports left on a table. And that was the so-called border control!'

The real culture shock for many young Brits came in going behind the Iron Curtain. In 1985 Tony Fielding took an Inter-Railing trip with friends through Yugoslavia, Rumania and Hungary. 'You instantly noticed the difference as you travelled into the Communist bloc. For starters, a lot of the train guards were accompanied by armed soldiers as they checked your passes. We saw a lot of funny sights, like in Hungary one day we were sitting down to enjoy a goulash overlooking the Danube when all these amphibious tanks started emerging from the river in our direction. It didn't exactly help the appetite! But the most bizarre place of all was Rumania which was still under Ceaucescu's regime at the time. As we neared the border through the swirling mists of Transylvania, the Rumanian family with whom we'd been chatting since Budapest urged us to refrain from laughing. At the border itself we were woken by Ian Fleming's 'Olga Klebb.' She was accompanied by a serious-looking guard carrying a machine gun and proceeded to exact an overpriced visa fee from us and made us buy a certain amount of Rumanian currency immediately. We later found out that there was next to nothing to spend your money on once in Rumania.

'During the day in Bucharest we saw no other Western tourists. What we did see a lot of were crumbling buildings and roads melting in the heat. We were followed the whole time by men in ill-cut suits. We managed to spend some of the money we'd been forced to exchange on postcards, stamps and glue to stick the stamps on, as the stamps themselves didn't have adhesive. All this was from a grocery shop which seemed to sell little more than a few jars of pickles, faded in the shop window and some rancid milk.

Above: Jerry Green's inter-rail adventures included a shrinking Greek train.

Opposite top: Round-the-world air tickets opened up exotic destinations, such as Hawaii, for those travelling on a budget.

Opposite bottom: Tony Fielding (right) 'wanted to see Europe but didn't have much money.' Inter-rail was the answer.

BACKPACKING AND BEACHPARTIES

We finished the day eating fish and chips, sharing a table in a restaurant with a family of four, all of whom except the father was blind. The father made the most of his gifted status by surreptitiously ordering cocktails throughout the meal. At the end, it was no surprise to find that this poor-looking family had insufficient money to cover their bill, including cocktails, so we chipped in to help. We knew we would be able to do very little with our money in Bucharest before we left that night. The whole experience was funny and sad in equal measure and by the time we arrived at the station to leave, we found it plunged into darkness. They did that every night apparently, to save money. Imagine King's Cross at rush hour with hundreds of people milling around and no lights on. By then we had realised that in Rumania the bizarre was the norm.'

Independent youth travel was transformed by a revolution in the travel industry which brought about the availability of cheap airfares, affordable to young people. Economy class air tickets were only introduced at the end of the 1950s. When the Boeing 747 and the new generation of jumbo jets were introduced in the 1970s, airlines could carry 500 people on flights which previously had only managed 150. They were more than doubling up on capacity but were unable to attract sufficient passengers as the fares were set by IATA and were prohibitively expensive – outside the reach of ordinary passengers let alone students. Rather than having empty planes, the airlines sought a way of selling off their remaining tickets. They couldn't offer cheaper unofficial fares alongside the standard extortionate ones as no-one would then buy the normal tickets and it would undermine the established markets. The solution was to find other agencies in back streets in Soho to sell the tickets at unofficial rates and fill up the flights. In this way the bucket shop was born and a system developed of offloading leftover seats. A lot of the bucket shops sold tickets to immigrants who were returning home on a visit to India, Pakistan and the Far East. From the early 80s onwards large numbers of students and twenty-somethings began latching onto these discounted flights to former colonies as an affordable and accessible way of seeing the world outside Europe. A discounted flight to the East could be had for less than the price of a first class return from London to Glasgow.

Ann-Marie Evans had just graduated from Liverpool University in 1983 when she became a backpacker. 'I had always wanted to travel and see as much of the world as possible, and there was this feeling that I should do it before I got weighed down with a career. I spent nine months working in the print room of an engineering firm and as a temp at the Middlesex Hospital in London to save up the money to buy a ticket to South East Asia. I was the only one among my friends to do it. They all thought that I would end up losing out in the career stakes and there was a real sense at the time that employers disapproved of you taking a year off to go travelling. I ended up travelling from Indonesia through Singapore, Malaysia, Thailand and up to Northern India and Nepal on a ten dollar a day budget.'

It wasn't just new graduates who were taking time out to go travelling. After a decade in the workplace, Shona Harris from Bath left her job in 1992 to go around the world. 'I went straight to work at 16 and had been at the coal face ever since. I was

Above: Ann-Marie Evans travelled around South East Asia on a $10 a day budget.

just getting over a broken relationship and had sold a house and I thought I'd better go off travelling now before I'm too old or the moment has passed. At the time there wasn't anything much worth staying home for. When I left there was a great feeling of having escaped, and a lovely sense of freedom. I didn't have to answer to anybody or do any job, this time was just for me. The possibilities of all the things I could do were wonderful. In the end I spent a lot of time in Asia as I knew the money would last longer there.'

Doing everything on the cheap, in the most basic way possible, was one of the characteristics of the backpacker. Ann-Marie Evans remembers, 'I slept in dorms with 30 other people, I remember once staying in a hostel in India where I saw rats running up the stairs and I was bitten to bits by bedbugs in Nepal that managed to get through my sheet sleeping bag. Funnily enough, I didn't mind roughing it. There was something appealing about the simplicity of life, you didn't need much stuff to get by. And there was a real camaraderie with other travellers I met who were doing it the same way.'

Madeleine Ashton, who travelled around Europe and Asia in the late 80s, recalls there was an inverse snobbery amongst backpackers and even a source of pride about doing it on the cheap. 'We weren't cosseted tourists who went from air-conditioned buses to bland international hotels without ever getting a real flavour of the country we were in. Because we were doing it cheaply, using public transport along with all the locals, staying in basic places sometimes even in people's houses, we felt we were much more in touch with the local culture and definitely got to know people a lot better that way.'

Below: Women backpacking alone often find it safer to find a travelling companion along the way.

There was an unspoken rule amongst backpackers that the rougher the experience, the more genuine a traveller you were. Slumming it – say surviving 30 hour bus journeys in the searing heat while sharing a seat with a family of chickens and a pig – was a much more 'real' experience of a country than sleeping in the hibiscus-petal-strewn suite of a 5 star hotel. Backpackers claimed a moral superiority over the package holidaymaker whose safe, sanitised passage through a country prevented them from having an authentic experience of the place.

A new guidebook was launched that matched the backpacker's ethos of travelling on a shoestring. In 1982 the first *Rough Guide* was published. One of the authors Mark Ellingham, was fresh out of university and was travelling in Greece where he found that none of the guidebooks available dealt adequately with the budget traveller who wanted to have fun as well as gain an appreciation of the country they were visiting. 'There really wasn't a guidebook for me. There was nothing contemporary which had an enthusiasm for beaches and bars as well as ancient sites, which treated Greece as a 20th century living culture and which didn't make you feel inadequate for not having a lot of money.' *The Rough Guide to Greece* was the first to be published, followed by *Spain* and *Portugal*, all countries that were cheap and within easy reach. With the growing availability of cheap long haul flights, the *Rough Guides* were soon spanning the world. The series was popular with students and backpackers for its unstuffy approach to the areas it covered including

BACKPACKING AND BEACHPARTIES

information on cafes and restaurants where you stood a chance of meeting the local people rather than sticking to the safe tourist haunts, the aim being to get closer to the real country. It even had a social conscience which matched the political awareness of students of the era: the first *Rough Guide* was dedicated to Andreas Papandreou and his PASOK party, the Pan-Hellenic Socialist Movement. *Spain* was dedicated to the removal of all NATO military bases and the *Yugoslavia* guide was dedicated to a free, non-aligned and socialist state.

One of the challenges and excitements of independent travel was survival in a foreign country and a foreign culture with little money. Negotiating the pitfalls and coming through the disasters were an important part of the holiday. Many of the difficulties and dangers fell in fairly equal measure between young men and women – but women were especially targets for sexual harassment and violence. During the 1970s and 80s the greater freedom and equality encouraged by the women's movement meant that large numbers of young women were travelling the world in groups or, increasingly, by themselves. One problem they confronted was the assumption amongst lorry drivers in many countries that lone female hitch-hikers were fair game for casual sex. 'I hitched alone and a lot of lorry drivers would ask if free sex was part of the deal if they gave you a lift,' says Ginette Ruthven. 'Amazingly a polite "no, thanks" usually worked and they often ended up talking about all their relationship problems, so I felt like a therapist. It was only once I got beaten up and virtually raped by a couple of Yugoslavs in Italy, but I've experienced many more acts of kindness than cruelty.'

Many of the countries they visited upheld traditional, patriarchal attitudes towards women and young, female independent travellers were sometimes viewed as irreligious and immoral. They could be objects of desire, fascination, aggression and loathing for men, some of whom saw them as little different than prostitutes. This was the experience of Ann-Marie Evans, who travelled alone through South-East Asia in the early 80s. 'The fact that I had blonde hair used to attract lots of attention and by the time I'd been travelling a few months it was bleached virtually white. I dressed modestly but I still got a lot of unwanted attention. It was at its most difficult in the Muslim countries. In Kuala Lumpur, men grabbed my breasts and I got yelled at from car windows. I teamed up with an Australian woman so that we could keep an eye out for each other and look after each other's things.'

Many young women travellers were literally innocents abroad, still in their teens, on limited funds for their first big trip and therefore extremely vulnerable. The consequences could be disastrous as Helen Christopher discovered in 1991 when a dream trip backpacking around Mexico turned into a nightmare. 'I was just 17

Below: Travelling light and with time on their hands, backpackers can reach spots too remote for regular tourists.

at the time and avoiding going to university by spending a year working in New Zealand. On my way I stopped over in Mexico to travel around with friends. We spent some time on the beach in Puerto Escondido where I had my bumbag stolen. We were due to fly out from Acapulco and had to get the bus back there. Other backpackers had said that the bus was notorious for thefts and there were stories going around about bandits stopping the buses. I stuffed all my money into my bra for safekeeping and we embarked on the 8 hour night bus to Acapulco. It was pitch black travelling through the country and every so often the bus would stop to pick up more passengers. I dozed off only to wake when I found a bloke pushing himself against my leg. I gave him a filthy look and my male friend swapped seats with me.

Above: Wherever travellers went in South East Asia, there'd always be someone with their nose in the 'Lonely Planet', the backpacker's bible.

'The drama started shortly afterwards when a man went down to the front and held a gun against the driver's head. The bus pulled off onto the side of the road, the hijacker's accomplices ordered all the men off the bus where they had to lie face down in the road with guns waved over them. All the women were shunted up to the front except for us three European girls who were crowded into a double seat. I had all my money taken from me. The two other girls, who were sisters, were taken to the back of the bus. One of them had a gun against her head. She was raped, her sister too. The horror went on for about half an hour. The worst thing was not knowing what to do. They were shouting at us, but we didn't know what they were saying, we had no idea about what was the best way to behave in that situation. Then the male passengers were allowed back on and we carried on to Acapulco. We didn't tell the police about the rapes, by then we just wanted to leave, we didn't want to be examined. We didn't get much help from the British consul. He was in a posh hotel and only kept minimal hours. My friends went through pregnancy tests, AIDS tests and the difficulty of everyone knowing what had happened to them. I was traumatised. Still now I won't travel by bus abroad at night. And I have problems going to the cinema, the torches the ushers use bring it all back to me.'

Some young travellers actually thrived on risk and danger on their holidays and this led to the development of another new trend in independent youth travel, that of adventure holidays. These were the Generation X travellers, who sought adrenaline highs to take them away from the banality of normal life. In the 1980s and 90s there was a huge increase in adventure travel. Bungee jumping, white-water rafting, rock climbing, sky diving and jet-skiing were all extreme sports sought out by youngsters who wanted excitement on their travels. Mark Hooker, a carpenter from Devon, travelled through Central and South America in the early 90s in search of thrills. 'I had always wanted to go climbing and the further away I found myself from civilisation the better. My heroes were great explorers and achievers like Ernest Shackleton and Edmund Hillary. I ended up in Costa Rica after climbing in the Andes

BACKPACKING AND BEACHPARTIES

and was relaxing with some surfing. That's where I did my first bungee jump. The adrenaline rush was phenomenal, it was better than any drug I've ever done. Afterwards I got a job helping out with bungee jumps in return for a free one every so often. It was a good way of pulling the girls, you give them the thrill of their lives. I came home from Costa Rica with a wife.' By the 1990s tens of thousands of motivated young people like Mark had figured out that they could, with a little disposable income, share in the thrills. 'The feeling of absolute freedom, of accidentally on purpose seeking out some peril and living through it was compelling. It was certainly far better than being stuck in an office and slowly dying.'

Sadly, the feeling common to many backpackers that they were invincible and somehow protected because they were on holiday could prove to be fatal. In 1999 19 people were killed in the Swiss Alps whilst canyoning, the practice of abseiling and jumping down waterfalls, one of the most recently developed adrenaline sports to feature on adventure trips.

By the turn of the century a year off before or after university had become such an established part of student life that it had acquired a new name 'the gap year'.

Above: Rather than limiting themselves to Europe, gap year students now set their sights on long haul destinations.

Whereas in the past if you had announced that you wanted to take a gap year you might have been accused of wasting your time now it was positively encouraged as a good thing to do, an opportunity to develop some independence, discover other talents and nurture new skills. Reena Thakrar, a student at Bristol University, took a gap year in the late 1990s after her A levels. 'I wanted a break from full-time education and I also wanted to travel. I come from quite a sheltered background and this was a way of experiencing the real world, the ideal opportunity before the pressures of getting onto the career ladder. I worked in a newsagents to save up the money and then went to Hong Kong to teach English to children. I also travelled around a bit and worked in an orphanage in the Philippines. It was a wonderful experience, I wanted to give something back but it also gave me a lot.' Employers began to look favourably upon the gap year and according to a survey carried out in 1997, 87% of employers thought that new graduates who had taken a gap year would make better, more mature employees. By the late 1990s more than 20% of students were taking a year off with Australia the favourite destination. In 1999 alone over a hundred thousand young Brits visited Australia, many arriving on year-long working holiday visas which allowed them to work while travelling around. Australia offered them the advantage of a common language, a lingering anglicised culture and an abundance of casual work.

There were two ways of doing the gap year. Young people either spent time at home doing casual unskilled work like shelf-stacking for part of the year to save up the

Above: Bungee jumping is just one of the holiday adventures which gives an adrenaline rush some see as similar to taking drugs.

money, then spend it on the big trip, or they took a job abroad. With the latter the opportunities included teaching English in the Far East, picking olives in Greece, fruitpicking, environmental, conservation and community work, waitressing and barwork, living and working on a kibbutz or doing a season as a chalet girl or boy in the ski resorts of the Alps. The nature of a gap year was becoming more and more structured, less about dropping out from education and work and more about making positive moves that might impress future employers and fill out a CV. Increasingly, students were doing voluntary jobs that might improve their future careers: history students were going on archaeological digs, would-be teachers were getting an early experience of teaching and language students were brushing up on their linguistic skills abroad before embarking on a degree course. Reena Thakrar, a politics student says, 'I would like to work for the Foreign Office in future so it was fascinating being in Hong Kong after the handover. I am really pleased I did a gap year. It made me so much more confident and independent and when I started university it was easier to make friends having done the same thing on the other side of the world. It didn't take me long to adapt to life as a student and I'm sure that's because I'd already had the experience of adapting to a very different lifestyle in the Far East.'

By the mid-1990s the established backpacker's route went global as round-the-world tickets tumbled in price with airlines merging into global entities. Student and youth travel agency STA travel sent half a million young Brits abroad in 1999, many of them on round-the-world tickets. The trail was at its most well-trodden in Asia. The

BACKPACKING AND BEACHPARTIES

format was start in India, go trekking in Nepal, relax on a beach in Goa or Kerala, then follow the route through South-East Asia in Laos, Vietnam, Cambodia, Thailand (where the number of visitors has increased 64-fold since 1960), enjoy the Full Moon beach party scene on Ko Pha Ngan, then island-hopping in Indonesia, over to Darwin in Australia and then travel south to Sydney stopping on the Great Barrier Reef for some scuba diving and r 'n' r after the rigours of Asia. This route became so familiar that it was nicknamed the 'banana pancake' trail after the eponymous breakfast favoured by young backpackers. Together with other set pieces of the 'year out' like bungee-jumping in New Zealand and white-water rafting on the Zambezi the youth of the 1990s created the Generation X version of the classical 'Grand Tour.'

In recent years the independence of youth travel has come under threat not from outside forces but from the backpackers themselves. Instead of exploring new places, backpackers have been accused of heading like sheep for the travellers' ghettos of cheap hostels, cafes, fast-food joints and internet/phone/fax shops and voluntarily alienating themselves from the local culture and people of the countries they are in, preferring the company of fellow travellers. The present generation of travellers relied on the popular guidebooks, in particular the *Lonely Planet*, the bible of backpacking, to reinforce this sense of institutionalised tourism. Madeleine Ashton observes, 'It's unbelievable the way you can go just about anywhere now in Asia and everyone under 35 has their nose stuck in the *Lonely Planet*. So everyone ends up staying in the same places and eating at the same restaurants.'

Mike Jordan, a backpacker in his late 20s who has spent time in Thailand, doesn't have a problem with that. 'Basically I went there to have fun. It was a break from work and I didn't really want to spend it looking at some dull old monument, I wanted to meet up with like-minded people, sit on the beach, chill out and party.'

Dr Heba Aziz from the University of Surrey surveyed a backpacker's community while studying the Bedouins in Egypt. She discovered, 'The travellers were living in their own bubble. They remained exclusively in beachside cafes which offered identical menus. Egyptian food was nowhere to be found. Rather than being interested in the history and culture of the place, they could have been anywhere in the world. They have long been depicted as non-conformist travellers – the ones who wanted to mix with the local culture. But few of the backpackers in Dahab encountered local people in a non-commercial setting.' Backpackers, far from being conscientious, culture-seeking explorers were in danger of turning into that creature they sneered at – the package holidaymaker.

Beach holidays have also changed for the younger generation and it was Club 18-30 that started the revolution. When Club 18-30 was founded in 1965 the youth travel market was virtually non-existent – students went backpacking and other young people went on holiday with their parents. It was developed as a way of filling unpopular midweek flights with people who could get away during the week. The first season was on the Costa Brava. And the mid-60s turned out to be a good time to launch a holiday devoted to young people. The Club's founder was David Heard, 'It tapped into a rich vein. It was the swinging 60s and the first time young people had disposable income.' The holidays were promoted under the slogan; 'Holidays Your Granny Wouldn't Like' and appealed to those youngsters who were living at home with their parents and yearning for some freedom. But even though early advertising campaigns titillated the holidaymaker with hints of sexual explicitness, the reality was rather tame. Keith Byrne from Manchester, a Club 18-30 rep in the 1970s, remembers taking holidaymakers on trips to see at least two churches a week. Club 18-30 then was more of a junior, livelier version of the package holiday in the popular resorts of the Spanish Costas, and the Balearic and Greek islands.

David Heard remembers the turning point 'Of course, people got drunk and had sex – we didn't invent that. But there was a seminal point when the culture changed in 1970 and there was institutionalised rowdyism. An Australian rep decided the easiest option was to get people drunk. As opposed to going out and having a good time and incidentally getting drunk, he was doing it on excursions that didn't need it.' Club 18-30 holidaymakers were soon banned from the usual resort excursions. 'We were not allowed on the coaches because people threw up so we had to invent our own trips, which is how the beach barbecues and buggy safaris came about.' The drinking games became infamous and rumours of a lager lout culture spread.

Club 18-30 holidays were sold as 'fun in the sun' holidays and attracted the attention of the tabloid press who found drunken lads willing to boast of their sexual exploits. The tone of the press coverage had a knock-on effect and the sun, sea and sex image meant the Club attracted large groups of young men. Paul Riches, a rep in Spain during the early 1980s recalls, "In Magaluf there were running battles in the street. There were four or five weeks a season when 80-90% of the clients were men. One week I had 99 blokes and one girl in a hotel. The woman was the girlfriend of one of the lads and didn't come out all week.'

Then in the 1990s, one of the Spanish islands emerged as the party capital of Europe. Until the 1980s Ibiza was known as one of those package holiday destinations, a Blackpool-on-the-Med for sun and sangria worshippers. It had long attracted hedonist bohemians. A legacy from the Franco era, they came to Ibiza to escape the draconian regime which wouldn't even allow couples to kiss in the streets. These hippie residents set the tone and in the 1970s a club scene started to emerge with Euro-style discos becoming popular. In the heyday of one of the clubs, Pacha, the glitterati coming to groove included Ringo Starr, Harrison Ford, Roman Polanski and Ursula Andress.

By the mid-80s the drug ecstasy was starting to make in-roads into youth culture and fuse with house music to create the clubbing scene. British DJs went out to Ibiza,

This spread: Club culture has transformed Ibiza's image to that of the 'party capital of the world.'

BACKPACKING AND BEACHPARTIES

liked what they saw and started Mediterranean versions of their own clubs at home. The combination of music, drugs and the potent effects of sunshine on young hormones proved to be a major draw. Word got back to Britain of the party scene, of all-night clubbing and soon gangs of young Brits started going out for no-holds-barred hols of easy drugs and casual sex. As one bouncer put it, 'There are three brands of British tourist here – the lads on the beer, the lads on the pull and the lads on the pills.' Kevin McDonald, a joiner from Belfast went in a group of six male friends in the summer of 95. 'Ibiza was like one big party, one big club all the time. Everyone was young and there were lots of girls in skimpy tops so the hormones went into overdrive. Everyone was sleeping around, there were no inhibitions, it was really the best place I've ever been.'

For Kevin and his mates the days were spent building up to the big night out. 'We didn't really do much during the day. We'd get up around lunchtime and sit on the beach for a while to look at the topless girls or dander around the shops. Some blokes would deliberately try to set light to the fields with their lighters for a bit of a crack. The grass was dead dry and there were signs warning you not to smoke in them. Other guys would grab a scooter and go joy-riding in the afternoon. There were lots of accidents, young girls who've never been on a motorbike in their lives were falling off. We'd all get back to the apartment around six for dinner, usually a takeaway, and then we'd play cards and drink until we were really pissed and throw deckchairs off the balcony. Most nights we'd go into town around midnight. It was hectic, all the reps were trying to get you into their clubs. They'd chat you up and snog you just to get you in and give you a free drink and then leave you at the bar. We'd end up going to about 10 discos a night. At 4 a.m. foam came down from the ceiling and you'd dance in it 'til you were soaked.'

And it was just as wild for the girls. Trish James, a twenty-something sales manager, went to Ibiza in 1998 with her friend Louise. 'We were there about two weeks and between us we had about 30 blokes. Out of those, probably only about a third were worth the effort. What I got from the holiday was one big party every night, go out on the pull, have a good time, let our hair down and that's it. Every night the same thing. People on their hols want to let their hair down, at home they're more controlled, but you know, you don't shit on your own doorstep.'

Tiffany Parker from Bristol was just 16 when she went on a family holiday to Ibiza with her older cousins in 1997. 'There was a lot of pressure on me from my cousins to have a good time. And that basically meant get drunk as much as possible, stay out as late as possible and shag as many blokes as possible. I got dragged into it. We were too young to get into the clubs but we used to go down to a bar in San Antonio and people would pair off and go into the toilets to do it or down on the beach. By the end of the fortnight I still hadn't pulled, so my cousin poured a lot of alcohol down me and I

This spread: 'The party capital of the world' has always attracted more than its fair share of colourful characters.

ended up going into the toilets with this bloke. It was a dreadful experience.'

Ibiza had become a byword for hedonism. One club, the Manumission, was staging live sex shows and television series like *Ibiza Uncovered* revealed the excesses of young holidaymakers, enticing even more to go to the clubbers' cult resort. In 1998 the British vice-consul on the island, Michael Birkett, resigned in disgust at the antics of his young compatriots. By the end of the 20th century nearly a million young Britons were visiting Ibiza during the summer season and drugs with a street value of £200 million were being sold annually to the young ravers. Paradoxically for such a relatively small island, those parts of Ibiza outside of San Antonio or Ibiza town remain quiet and peaceful, untouched by the club culture.

As far as youth tourism is concerned, however, the new movement to hedonism has become all-pervasive. Whether it be backpacking or beach holidays, sex and drugs are now much higher up the agenda. The adrenaline rush induced by risk, danger and adventure has also become ever more important in independent travel holidays, but perhaps the greatest influence on this holiday sector has been the introduction of new technology. The computer age, the internet and the World Wide Web have changed the face of travel and young people have been more open to these changes than any other group. For them hotmail is replacing postcards and internet travel outfits like lastminute.com are the bucket shops of the new century. Many of these developments seem shocking to the older generations who were brought up on holidays at Blackpool and Butlins, booked many months in advance, or who came to believe that a two-week package on the Costa Blanca was the last word in summer fun. But the extremes of behaviour indulged in by young people today remain part of a well-established holiday tradition of escape,

entertainment and excess that stretches back to the beginning of the last century and beyond – simply the latest expression of the carefree attitude of the British on holiday at home and abroad.

FURTHER READING

Addison, Paul. *Now the War is Over: A Social History of Britain 1945-51*. London, J.Cape, 1985.

Akhtar, Miriam & Humphries, Steve. *Far Out, The Dawning of New Age Britain*. Bristol, Sansom & Co. 1999.

Brendon, Piers. *Thomas Cook: 150 Years of Popular Tourism*. Secker and Warburg, 1991.

Brown, Mick. *The Spiritual Tourist*. London, Bloomsbury, 1998.

Butlin, Sir Billy. *The Billy Butlin Story*. London, Robson Books, 1982.

Dass, Ram. *Be Here Now*. San Cristobal, New Mexico, Lama Foundation, 1971.

Fagg, Christine. *The Caravan Book – A Guide to Adventure and Fun on Wheels*. Watford, Exley Publications, 1982.

Fenton, Mike. *Camp Coach Holidays on the GWR*. Didcot, Wild Swan Publications,1999.

Gregory, Alexis. *The Golden Age of Travel*. London, Cassell, 1991.

Hudson, Simon. *Snow Business*. London, Cassell, 2000.

Humphries, Steve. *A Secret World of Sex*. London, Sidgwick and Jackson, 1988.

Jenkinson, Andrew. *Caravans: British Trailer Caravans 1919-1959*. Dorchester, Veloce Publishing, 1998.

Lea, Timothy. *Confessions from a Holiday Camp*. London, Sphere Books, 1972.

McAuley, Rob. *The Liners*. London, Boxtree, 1997.

Pimlott, J.A.R. *The Englishman's Holiday*. London, Faber & Faber, 1947.

Pressnell, Jon. *Touring Caravans*. Princes Risborough, Shire Publications Ltd, 1991.

Raitz, Vladimir and Bray, Roger. *Flight to the Sun*. London, Continuum Publishing Group, 2000.

Read, Sue. *Hello Campers*. London, Bantam Press, 1986.

Robb, John. *The Nineties, What the F**k was that all about?* London, Ebury Press, 1999.

Urry, John. *The Tourist Gaze*. London, SAGE, 1998.

Walton, JK. *The British Seaside: Holidays and resorts*. Manchester University Press 2000.

Walton, JK. *Blackpool*. Edinburgh University Press, 1998.

Walton, JK. *The Blackpool Landlady*. Manchester University Press, 1978.

Ward, Colin & Hardy, Dennis. *Goodnight Campers*. London, Mansell Publishing, 1986.

PICTURE CREDITS

© **Advertising Archives** 82 (left and middle), 90 (bottom), 94 (left), 112.

© **Allsport** 171.

© **Andrew Rapacz** 116 (right), 117.

© **Ann Ronan Picture Library** 14 (top), 16 (both), 17 (right), 19 (bottom), 28 (bottom), 152, 154, 155 (top).

© **Allsport** 171.

© **Blackpool Tourism Department** 34, 35.

© **Boeing** 106 (top).

© **Butlin's** 2 (bottom right), 8 (right), 38, 39, 40 (middle), 41 (top), 42 (top), 43 (programmes), 44, 45 (top), 46 (bottom), 52 (top), 53.

© **Center Parcs, Sherwood Forest** 51 (top).

© **Chris Fairclough Colour Library** 12 (right), 67, 68, 79, 103 (bottom), 106 (bottom), 111 (top), 116 (top), 119, 121, 122, 127 (middle), 144 (top), 168.

© **Club Med** 51 (bottom).

© **David Beare** 3, 103 (top), 109 (top).

© **David Burgess-Wise** 70 (top), 74 (left), 76.

© **Dinodia Picture Agency** 135 (insert), 141, 167.

© **Egan Family** 10 (bottom).

© **Eastbourne Tourism & Leisure Department** 10, 15.

© **Hulton Getty** 7, 9, 13, 32, 54, 55 (bottom right), 57, 58 (top), 19, 20, 24, 78, 84, 88, 89, 91, 92 (top left and bottom), 97, 156.

© **Joan Pollock** 136 (top).

© **Meribel** 159 (left).

© **Peters Collection donated to the Bournemouth *Daily Echo*** 12 (left), 17 (top and bottom left).

© **Rex** 132 (top), 136 (bottom) 137, 138, 139, 140, 142 (right), 143, 144, 146 (left and top middle), 148.

© **Spanish Tourist Authority** 50 (top).

© **Still Pictures** 163 (top).

© **The Hop Farm, Kent** 65 (top), 66 (bottom).

©**Thomas Cook Archives** 94 (right), 96 (top), 102 (top), 104, 105, 107, 150 (top).

© **Towner Art Gallery & Local Museum Eastbourne** 14 (bottom), 15, 18.

© **Virgin Atlantic** 170.

Agency pictures researched by Image Select International.

The remaining pictures were sourced from private collections. Special thanks to: Madeleine Ashton, Pete Bradshaw, Simon Buchanan, Lloyd and Lyn Brown, Margaret Butcher, Ron Callow, Marjorie Chalker, Eileen Cook, Ann-Marie Evans, Chris Fawcett, Christine Fagg, George Field, Tony Fielding, John Gardner, Stuart Gillespie, Eve Green, Jerry Green, Mary Greenhough, Sallie Haddon, Chris Hall, Shona Harris, Melissa Harrison, Barbara Holman, the Hornby sisters, Tim Hunt, Dorothy Isles, Irene Jackson, Derek Johnson, Jacquie Kilty, Stan and Dave Little, Pat Mancini, Alan Marsden, Lucy and Perry Mason, Margaret Maudsley, Mike McGregor, Ed Mitchell, Gladys and Buster Nuttall, Ann Preen, Josephine Roffey, Geoffrey Smith, Lola Smith, Reena Thakrar, Kathy Vyse, Rene Wilkins, Pamela Woodland, John Wyllie.